7 THINGS
YOUR
TEENAGER
WON'T
TELL
YOU

7 THINGS YOUR TEENAGER WON'T TELL YOU

—and How to Talk About Them Anyway

Jenifer Marshall Lippincott
and Robin M. Deutsch, Ph.D.

BALLANTINE BOOKS TRADE PAPERBACKS
NEW YORK

To Rob, Anabel, and Tess,
my inspiration in all things adolescent—and otherwise.
And to my parents, who continue to guide me—every day.

....

For Marcia and RK, who took me through adolescence;
Larry, who accompanied me out;
and Emma and Sam, who give it new meaning.

ACKNOWLEDGMENTS

Thanks to all the generous participants in our focus groups without whom so many ideas would not have come to life. And to the stellar group of neuropsychologists, in particular Suzanne Dowdall, for their consulting assistance on the adolescent brain.

To Rob Dunn, Neva Egloff, DJ Hynes, Emma Miller, and Lindsay Symes for such honest and lustrous perspective on their own adolescence and the parents who guided them through it.

Thanks to Doe Coover, our agent, for her acute insights, professional deftness, and friendship.

To Elisabeth Dyssegaard and Jill Schwartzman, our editors, for their strength of purpose, focus, and patience as they ushered us through this process.

To Caroline Sutton, who jumped aboard at full speed and was instrumental in guiding the book to fruition. She not only listened, she heard.

To Marisa Vigilante for grabbing the baton with such gusto and to Shona McCarthy for her expert production editing.

Thanks to Jesseca Salky for her energy, dedication, and sense of direction in setting the book in motion.

—Jenifer and Robin

Thank you to Susan Edbril and Jodi Davenport for showing me the way and then being there at every turn.

To Jess Brallier and Sara Hunter for the encouragement that let me believe.

To Marty, John and Katy Henderson, Marcia Trook, Erika Guy, Beth Rendeiro, and Claudia Wallis for their enthusiasm, support, and generosity.

To Donna Marshall Constantinople and Nick Constantinople whose devotion and humor as they raised three adolescent daughters to near perfection were an inspiration to me—and models to us all.

To Maura Marshall and Marsh Marshall for being the staunch yet welcoming pillars on whom I perpetually lean, whether they know it or not.

And to Robin Deutsch whose wisdom, insight, and voice of reason allow her to stand tall in a field of giants. She listened to a mere sketch of a dream, agreed to pursue it with me, and ended up enabling its reality. I am so grateful.

To my adolescents, Anabel and Tess, who embody the raw perfection of a crystal-clear dawn with the promise to warm the entire earth. If only I could live up to the lessons you have taught me.

Finally, to my husband, Rob, who tirelessly, cheerfully, and selflessly took on every conceivable role in support of this effort, from reader to editor, from advisor to guinea pig, from office support to tech support. Every word in this book, even before it was written is, in some way, because of you.

—Jenifer

Many people have provided encouragement and support for this book. I thank in particular my late colleague Ken Herman, who taught me how to listen to the voices of children and adolescents.

I am grateful for the opportunity to work with so many adolescents and parents, who have shared their lives and taught me so much. Though none of my patients' stories appear in this book, listening to their perspectives has helped me better understand how parents and adolescents can hear each other.

I am deeply grateful to Jenifer, who seeded our collaboration. Since she brought me into this project, my immense respect and admiration for her keen insight, critical thinking, and creativity have only grown. Developing this book and our friendship in tandem has been a remarkable experience.

I thank my children, Emma and Sam, who supported me, trusted that I would not misrepresent their needs or views, and gave me the opportunity to experience the best of adolescence. And I am indebted to my husband, Larry Miller, who listened to and supported me, steadfastly believing that this book would make a difference.

—Robin

CONTENTS

PART I

Our Jobs Redefined

INTRODUCTION

THE ESSENCE OF ADOLESCENCE HASN'T CHANGED SINCE THIS book was first published in 2005. Their brains haven't skipped a growth spurt; their search for identity hasn't been called off, or even detoured; they haven't forgotten how to speak with the ease of attitude.

And yet, fingers fly across keys to a host of new adolescent domains—from texting to iTunes, from chats to anything-on-demand. Within a few short years, instant messaging and search engines metastisized into billions of stampeding text cells, emasculated the benefits of delayed gratification, shrank the globe, harnessed time, redefined the word social, and ushered in a host of adolescent torments—from cyberbullying to new forms of sexual exploitation or worse, harassment. We compete for mindshare, boats against increasingly strong currents of stimuli that are constantly grabbing for our adolescent's attention as we pursue our own form of parenting manifest destiny.

The enemy of focused thinking is distraction. And the dashboard of the adolescent cockpit is a veritable arcade of them. Homework wedges in between chats or other online adventures. The *ping* of a new text message or a change of song on a playlist yanks any brief foray into deeper thought back to the surface. A must-see YouTube movie demands immediate commentary, while unwatched episodes of favorite TV shows stack up, beckon.

As parents, we know things instinctively: the benefits of sleep, reading, a carefully negotiated treat. We know things deep down where no one else can get to or feel. That place that awakens us before our adolescents do, alerts us before a blow, sorts cares from worries, truth from fiction. We parent to its churn, its hum, wallow in its triumphs, absorb its disappointments. Yet, revelations about the teenage brain continue to shed new light on learning, addiction, the importance of sleep, the ability to cope, the impact of endless hours of wireless pleasure. New studies reveal strongholds of stress eating away at already fragile adolescent equlibria, begetting a new genre of anxiety disorders. Or brains rewiring themselves beneath our, their teachers' and even admissions officers', noses. The result of days' worth of hours fixated on a screen. New data about teen drinking, pregnancy, even how they think about us, help us keep them in perspective and keep them drawn to us like whirling planets to the sun.

Plus ça change, plus c'est la même chose. The more things change, the more they stay the same.

> **THEM:** *You wanted me?*
> **US:** *Yes, I wanted to know how it went.*
> **THEM:** *Fine.*
> **US:** *Fine?*
> **THEM:** *Yes, fine. Can I go now?*
> **US:** *Wait. You haven't told me anything.*
> **THEM:** *What? What do you want to know?*
> **US:** *Well . . . what did they say?*

THEM: *Look, I'm in the middle of something. Can we talk about this later?*
US: *What are you in the middle of? What's so important? Why can't you just answer one question?*
THEM: *Why are you freaking out? I'm trying to tell you!*

Sometimes, the conversations with our adolescents sound soothingly familiar, like verses of an oldie but goodie. Sometimes they sound like a foreign language that we speak but don't comprehend, like venom we swore to ourselves we would never spew.

Inexorably, these conversations guide *us* as we guide *them*, pushing each other up the child-rearing mountain—two steps forward and three back, sometimes the other way around—toward a summit where we hope to at least glimpse their adulthood. Breathless from the changes, both internal and external, theirs and ours, we pause, sometimes reluctantly, to acknowledge our parents' voices in our own.

Meanwhile, our job remains to bear the brunt, dodge aimless shards of frustration, redirect intentions, while they, to paraphrase Aristotle, learn how to be angry/happy/sad at the right person to the right degree at the right time for the right purpose and in the right way.

To our adolescents, conversations with us are often embellished requests or rationalizations. To us, these conversations are less a utilitarian transfer of information than our best opportunity to understand and monitor that temperamental and mysterious organism called the adolescent. So often, conversations with our adolescents feel as strong as a three-run lead—and as easily shattered by one bad play. Often, we don't stop to analyze the many aborted conversations with them; there are just too many, and we are too busy hauling our adolescents (and often their siblings) up that incline. Of course, the dangerous precipices we know, like driver's licenses and steady relationships, appear tame compared to those we don't, like the magnetic attraction of the online world. Suddenly, the adolescent slope appears a lot slipperier than we realized, the brinks a lot closer.

Should we let her go to the party? How much is too much time on the computer? Do they really need to send hundreds of texts a day? Can they really do three things at once and do a good job on homework? We fire dilemmas into our inner sanctums with no real aim, in hopeful search of a sign. The gut is a sieve of values and emotion through which we sort millions of bits of information, memory, experience. Yet we let the conscious mind do our bidding.

In the end, a lot of parenting is pretty ad hoc, driven by fantasy or fear, reaction rather than proaction. Regardless of their origin, for words to stick, they have to sound right when we utter them and land where our adolescents can receive them. Even then, there are no guarantees. We struggle to interpret, keep up, filter, unclutter. As their language changes, so must ours.

This book presents a new way of thinking about conversations as the gateway into our teenagers' worlds. Through conversation, we are as easily barred as granted access to their often secretive but rarely impenetrable thoughts. We just need the right passwords for entry—and the right techniques to keep the communication lines open and constructive.

We base our ideas about how to keep the adolescent conversation going on more than sixty (combined adult) years of listening to—and in some cases eavesdropping on—the everyday realities of family life, classroom interactions, juvenile court proceedings, therapy sessions, focus groups, dinner party conversations, and soccer sideline chats. This anecdotal evidence can be sorted into two different types of conversations:

the ones *between* our adolescents and us, and the ones between us and other adults *about* our adolescents. Both sets of sources confirm that certain subjects, or themes, seem to scuttle even the best-intentioned conversation en route to a logical explanation. These themes, and all they entail—honesty, drugs and alcohol, sex, self-image, media technology, friends, and power struggles—are also the subjects that try a parent's soul.

This book revolves around these seven things that we believe govern adolescents' lives. Listen in on the conversations between the parents of adolescents, and likely as not one of these themes will surface.

> **US:** *I know he's getting high a lot, but if his father [or teachers, or coach] knew, he'd kill him. Of course, when I confront him, he just denies it. After all we've done for him, I can't believe he would do this to us.*

So what are the passwords that will secure conversational access to our adolescents? They are seven simple statements that reveal the very things our adolescents don't necessarily want us to know, but we need to anyway—in order to keep the conversation going.

SEVEN THINGS YOUR TEENAGER WON'T TELL YOU
(*And How to Talk About Them Anyway*)

1. Their brains are to blame.

2. Truth is as malleable as their Friday night plans.

---

3. Controlling them is not the point.

4. The adolescent mirror distorts.

5. Friends don't matter as much as we may think.

6. When we say *no*, they hear *maybe*.

7. Taking risks gives them power.

So why these seven statements? Because they represent the often discordant, sometimes unpalatable, internal struggles of teenagers between the ages of eleven and eighteen. And because they support a large body of work by adolescent theorists who maintain that until adolescents can make reasonable judgments about these issues consistently on their own, they cannot divine a truly independent identity, an essential prerequisite for entry into adulthood.

Each of these seven statements may stick in our throats like an oversized pill until absorbed into whatever level of consciousness we can handle. Many of them may sound familiar. Others may ring false. Some may not be relevant—yet. Some may never be. But whether we like them or not, whether they are ready or not, our adolescents confront these truths daily. As adults, we can choose one of two perspectives: We can try to participate in their worlds, or we can pretend that they are living in ours.

This is a book that tells the truth about what to expect of our children's adolescence. It is a book about what *is* real, not what we *want* to be real about the world they live in. Whether these truths represent new insights or old ones, good or bad news, the question is: What can we do about them? And the answer is simple: Accept them. Like acne and attitude, they are part of the changing terrain of the adolescent landscape. Not every one of them for every adolescent. But the sooner we accept them as reality, the sooner we can get on with our real jobs as parents.

And what is a parent's real job during our children's adolescence? What it has always been: to keep them *safe, nourished,* and *sheltered.* Here's how we need to redefine these jobs.

JOB DESCRIPTIONS

THOUGH STILL RESPONSIBLE, WE ARE NO LONGER IN CHARGE of our adolescents. At least not entirely. Our window into their world is only as open as *they* want it to be. Sure, we sometimes catch glimpses without them noticing; we can even prop open the windows from time to time. We also have levers, both tangible and intangible, such as money, privileges, transportation, gadgetry, guilt—and, most important, their continuing need for our approval—that can promote or curtail actions and behaviors. But these are merely job aids: temporary, time-sensitive, often adversarial solutions to be used judiciously and sparingly lest they lose their potency or enable duplicity. To perform our real jobs effectively requires our adolescents' complicity. They're either on board or they're not. They're either part of the resistance or our accomplices. It all depends on how we want to play it.

■ **Keep them safe.** Safe still means to keep them out of harm's way, though the dangers are no longer hot stoves and household poisons. Rather, physical, psychological, cyber, and social trip wires lie in their paths, each one threatening to impede, if not seriously delay, their progress toward maturity. And notice that they don't look back at us very often. On the contrary, they don't for a minute believe that they need our assistance anymore (though they may willingly, on occasion, accept a helping hand).

■ **Nourish them.** Though we will probably always remain their chief cooks and bottle washers, *nourishment* no longer applies only to food. There's a hunger now that runs deeper than the one that gnaws their empty stomachs. The adolescent appetite craves independence, power, experience, and—yes—pleasure. As always, however, our nourishment remains a primary source of their strength fed by an endless supply of comfort and acceptance. And from that strength comes the ability to make decisions, good or bad. This is the ability that we must nourish—while we still can. Like any new muscle, the decision-making ones require regular exercise with additional weight added incrementally as strength builds. Weak at first and easily tired, the decision-making muscles eventually develop their own unconscious competence.

■ **Shelter them.** Whether they're physically under our roofs or someone else's, we are and need to remain our adolescents' home base—always there, always ready to help, bail, respond. Just as each teenager is constructed differently, so we must construct his or her shelter. And just as our homes contain spaces to host specific activities, so must the shelters we provide them. There must be room for privacy, space belonging to them alone. There must also be room for contributing—or giving back. And, perhaps most important, there must be room to find and achieve success—the opportunity to strike that one pose that showcases their strengths, not their flaws. We may not always appreciate the extra piercing or visible underwear label or type of music ... or back talk. Nevertheless, our job is to provide a place where our adolescents can always find shelter. The one place where they always know they are welcome.

If we are updating *our* job descriptions, what about *theirs*? We don't need a psychology degree to see the molting process that's going on, literally before our eyes. And part of the resulting reconditioning requires that our adolescents prove to themselves—and to us—that they can make their own decisions, and that we, or at least our directions, are often wrong. In other words, their job is pretty much diametrically opposed to ours. And how exactly are we supposed to defy nature by convincing them that they are better off joining forces with us? The answer: Keep it simple and shoot straight. This is our best chance at keeping the conversations with our teenagers constructive and focused on a desired outcome.

Think of the things that our adolescents *don't want us to know* not as obstacles to overcome or threats to expose. They merely form the uneven, often unforgiving playing fields on which our adolescents stumble their way through conflicts and unfair calls and advantages. Our challenge is to teach them three basic plays—the golden rules of adolescence. We can coach from the sidelines, even call fouls and inflict penalties. What we can't do is play for them. We just convince them that if they stick to the three Rules of Play, they'll be headed toward the right goal.

THE RULES OF PLAY

IS IT POSSIBLE TO ACHIEVE LASTING PEACE DURING OUR CHILdren's adolescence under the guidance of only three commandments: stay safe; show respect; keep in touch? While these three simple rules may not guarantee a smooth ride through adolescence, they can ease some of the stresses that tend to ambush our teens—and us—as we all struggle toward (their) adulthood.

OUR OWN ADOLESCENCE—A LOOK BACK

THOUGH WE'VE ALL SEARCHED, FEW OF US HAVE FOUND A REliable way to hold a conversation with our adolescents that consistently evades conflict, or at least contention. Why is it so easy to forget that *we're* the grown-ups? Too often, the moment we detect static in the communication lines with our adolescents, we tend to rush to the defensive, either for protection or to rack up another parenting victory.

US: *Don't you speak to me in that tone of voice! Keep it up and you can forget your plans for the weekend.*

Meant as harmless pinpricks aimed at our adolescents' psyches, these types of ultimatums tend to choke off most conversations, leaving tempers smoldering.

THEM: *You can't do that! You know I already have plans. Why do you always have to spoil everything?*

This kind of conversational tack rarely heads in a positive direction.

Frazzled by these types of savaged conversations, we wonder why we are not entitled to wear the same cloak of respect as that of our parents. While theirs fit squarely upon shoulders that flaunted an air of unassailable power, that same cloak hangs awkwardly on us, out of style and ill fitting. Lest we forget, our parents ruled in a different kingdom, and many of us, as their subjects, were not always the loyal followers that they believed us to be.

Why aren't we able to engender the same obsequiousness in our adolescents as many of us conveyed to our parents? As products of a different era, we came of age in a time when the fruits of our parents' labors bought us, their offspring, the ultimate luxury—free time. Unleashed from the burden of contributing to family survival, we never questioned the leisurely pace with which we were allowed to saunter through our pre-adult years, urged to learn and explore to our heart's content, rewarded for any glory that showcased our parents' successes (however modest by today's standards).

Our parents, whether participants or direct descendants of a victorious postwar generation, led the charge to create a better one, decorated with opportunity, cushioned by heightened levels of comfort. Conceived in glory, we, as the lucky benefactors, were liberated from societal debts or struggle for anything but our own causes. And so we became the early adapters, the birthright members of a whole new era of adolescence. With a mandate to go forth and excel, we were fearless in our pursuit of our parents' promises.

Wanting for little, we searched for more and in doing so created loftier goals and even higher aspirations than a comfortable home, a car or two in the driveway, and the promise of a good education. Time and opportunity allowed us to both experiment and question. Through experimentation, we proved that boundaries confined only the meek. Better jobs, more money, higher pinnacles of success were all achievable. Through questioning, we discovered that nothing was sacrosanct, not our parents' authority, not the government, not even the law. Regardless of the degree of difficulty of our personal journeys through adolescence, we proved it to be a profitable investment for our parents, thereby entrenching it as a necessary and essential gateway to adulthood.

Why the history lesson? Perhaps to shed new light on why our adolescents think, act, and speak differently than we did. Perhaps because to change the future requires a fresh look at the past.

TODAY'S ADOLESCENT—WHAT'S CHANGED?

RAISED FROM BIRTH ON A NUTRITIOUS DIET OF ACTIVITIES, lessons, and above all encouragement, our teenagers seem to thrive as we escort them from one expectation to the next. Whether in school, on sports teams, via music lessons, or through countless other releases from tolls of responsibility except to excel, we strive, because we can, to eradicate any hindrances that could divert their focus from our intended outcomes. By heaping on copious praise for any effort or positive intention, rather than for jobs actually well done—by encouraging and engaging them to "use their words," to discuss, negotiate, and query, rather than practice and demonstrate— we may have entrenched our adolescents even further in an accountability abyss where their sole purpose is to do us proud. By removing a sense of usefulness at a time when they are struggling the hardest to define themselves, have we inadvertently cut off one of their natural sources of self-worth? What does it say about us that frequent articles in major newspapers cite incidents of parents employing "aggressive," "devious," even "fraudulent" tactics, all in the name of getting their kids into desired schools ranging from preschool to college? *Desired by whom?* we might ask. Where are the data connecting higher grades to success or, more important, contentment in life? What does it say about our adolescents when a recent study on the ethics of American youth finds that despite significant increases over the past ten years in lying, stealing, and cheating, 77 percent believe that they are "better than most people" they know when it comes to doing the right thing? (although 26 percent admitted to lying on at least one question on the survey.)[1] Perhaps we have done a better job of inflating their egos than bolstering their consciences or self-efficacy.

What do you want from me? we often hear them plead. *We want you to succeed,* we implore. *We want you to do your best, to feel good about yourself.* We want them to have had a happy childhood, we rationalize.

So we pledge anew to do whatever we can to enable their success. Too often, though, in our eagerness to pass on a legacy of parental generosity, we overlook the critical proteins of sacrifice and responsibility.

THEM: *Mom, c'mon, I'm late for school. I'll clean up my room when I get home.*
US: *That's what you said yesterday. You know our agreement is that you at least make your bed—before school. You also know that it's one of your responsibilities as a family member.*
THEM: *I know, I know. But do you want me to be late for school? I just didn't have time this morning. Cut me a break, why don't you?*

And so the dilemma goes:

■ No, we don't want them to be late for school (or miss out on any fun or opportunity that presents itself, especially if it could reflect badly on them or, worse, on us).

■ Yes, we are frustrated because this isn't the first or the fifth time or even the twenty-fifth time they've neglected a responsibility.

■ Yes, we are annoyed that they don't seem to understand that, in the grand scheme of things, straightening one's room is a very small task, and one of the few that's asked of them, but . . . (see next bullet).

■ Though this may not be a skirmish worth escalating into a full-on battle, any mutually agreed-upon responsibility should be accounted for. (As a matter of fact, a survey of 639 adolescents regarding their practices related to a host of adolescent issues, such as drinking, smoking marijuana, sex, eating, school performance, and more, found that one of the common denominators among the 12.5 percent who were "too good to be true" was a requirement that they keep their rooms clean. Other common denominators were frequent family dinners, intact family units, no phones in rooms, and some type of community service.)[2]

How do we deal with the plight of the long-term investment versus the short-term gain when it comes to raising our teenagers? What rules do we put in place that acknowledge the same loopholes we discovered, indeed created, in our parents' parenting, yet allow our adolescents to discover the benefit to their own self-image of even the smallest contribution?

The good news is that it is never too late to change our parenting practices. The better news is that it's simpler than we think.

THE CASE FOR THE RULES OF PLAY

TO UNDERSTAND, LET ALONE EMBRACE, THE RULES OF PLAY may require a shift in parental focus. We are all familiar with the many unenforceable restrictions designed to make us feel better—say, by letting us know where they are and what they're up to. The Rules of Play offer a different approach—and a very simple promise: to keep the conversation going.

> **THEM:** *I'll do it later! I promise. If I do it now, I'll be late for school, and it will be your fault!*
> **US:** *I don't want you to be late for school, or to get into trouble. But I do want you to live up to the responsibilities you've agreed to. Go to school. We'll continue the conversation when you get back. Bye, sweetie, enjoy your day!*

To enforce the Rules of Play, we neither fume nor forget; we just move on, grateful to avoid another no-win confrontation. We tuck away a possible consequence or two (for ideas, see chapter 3, Controlling Them Is Not the Point), and wait for the right time to resume the conversation (preferably before the incident fades entirely from our already overburdened brains).

> **US:** *You know, I've given our conversation this morning [or whenever] some thought and here's the deal . . .*

There is nothing like a cool head to calm a heated discussion.

We position the Rules of Play (stay safe, show respect, keep in touch), not us, as the arbiter of many a dispute or potential dispute. Used effectively, these three strategies can spare a multitude of wasted words, arguments, and bad feelings. Their success depends on *both* parties (parent and teenager) recognizing the simplicity, validity, and practicality of only three guiding principles: Stay safe. Show respect. Keep in touch. Our conversations need only reinforce them.

As we well know, a hallmark of adolescence is resistance. Just as crying exercises a baby's lungs, resistance exercises adolescents' abstract reasoning skills—and apparently their jawbones. No longer able to physically contain or comfort them, our only hope is to stay in touch. Will we encounter the usual crackling and interference and even disconnections? Absolutely. But rather than trying to prevail or curtail, we need only strive for the connection itself. To be connected is to have a relationship; what takes two to begin, takes only one to end.

To demonstrate quickly the flexibility of the Rules of Play, let's apply them to a variety of typical adolescent issues (further explanation of how each rule works continues throughout this chapter):

ISSUE	RULE(S) OF PLAY
A sibling altercation, an avoided chore	Show respect
Lying, cheating, stealing	Stay safe, show respect
Drinking, smoking, taking drugs	Stay safe, show respect
Broken curfew, driving with an inappropriate person(s), wrong place at the wrong time	Keep in touch, stay safe

When our adolescents uphold the three rules responsibly, we reward them with more freedom. With freedom comes responsibility. More responsibility earns more freedom. How do we know whether they are abiding by the Rules of Play? The only way we can: through conversation.

SELLING THE RULES OF PLAY TO OUR ADOLESCENTS

GETTING OUR TEENAGERS TO BUY INTO THE RULES OF PLAY requires the best sales pitch we may ever make. Some will sign on right away; others, for a host of mostly developmental reasons (see chapter 1, Their Brains Are to Blame), will force us to trudge up and over (and back up and over) a mountain of objections. Undaunted, we persist, convinced that we are laying the groundwork for a vital communication system: that's right, the Rules of Play. The pitch boils down to this:

US: *There are only three rules we ask you to abide by, and their sole purpose is simply to enable us (as your parents) to sleep at night. That's it! Stay safe, show respect, and keep in touch.*

So how do we get our adolescents to play by these three rules? Start by making sure that they understand the whys (and be prepared to explain them multiple times in multiple ways). We might have succeeded with the command–and–control method at a younger age, but no longer. During adolescence, our only hope for achieving peaceful settlements is by engendering respect and cooperation. Like most things we value highly, respect and cooperation must be earned, and there is only one way to do that: through actions, theirs and ours.

So what keeps you up at night? our adolescents might ask.

In a word, we confess, *worry. Parents, by their nature, worry.* (Admittedly a wretched affliction that invades the body upon the birth of the first child and torments us forever.)

Ridiculous! they say.

Yes, we admit. *But true.*

Well, that's your problem, not mine, they remind us.

Actually not, we cajole, *because the more I worry about you, the more my worry will affect you. So it's in your best interest to help minimize my concerns. That way I will sleep better and you'll have a better chance of getting what you want!*

How's that? they say, rolling their eyes.

Three simple ways, we repeat (and repeat and repeat and repeat): *Stay safe, show respect, and keep in touch.*

And how do we do that again? they intone. (Aha! They may even be listening . . .)

It's simple, we impress (again and again and again). *You need only abide by three simple rules,* we repeat (and repeat and repeat and repeat . . .)

Most adolescents will get the correlation fairly quickly between sleep deprivation and crankiness—and crankiness and a decreased willingness on our parts to go along with desired plans. For the more recalcitrant ones, a few detours placed on their critical paths should help nudge them along. An important key to rule adherence: enlightened self-interest.

In the end, there really aren't any consistently measurable criteria or prerequisites that guarantee a good adult–adolescent relationship. There is only the respect we demonstrate for the process and the connections that form as a result.

Rule #1: STAY SAFE

KEEP IN MIND THAT SINCE MOST ADOLESCENTS FEEL PRETTY invulnerable and not at all risk-averse, they will not necessarily share our concerns about safety. Safety—the single biggest source of worry for a parent—occupies its own hierarchy, with each level bleeding into the next:

I. Physical Safety

Physical safety, of course, means avoiding anything that could lead to or cause physical harm. Most of us can admit to being taken hostage by an endless string of threats to our children, real or imagined. Charged with enforcing their safety, but powerless to ensure it, we obsess about what could go wrong. Memories of our own pasts magnify the nightmarish possibilities confronting our adolescents, and yet we now face the same inability to control them that our parents faced. And while our parents often opted to look the other way, we often know too much to do so. Can we really expect our adolescents to bypass the bad decisions and forbidden fruits that we could not?

Perhaps the only way to teach our adolescents how to stay safe is to assume that they will inevitably find themselves in unsafe territory. So we constantly point out the dangerous curves and warn them to beware of a slippery choice. We methodically reiterate the many possible consequences of bad decisions as a reminder to us—and them—that complacency can never replace caution. This leads us to the next level in the *Stay Safe* hierarchy.

II. Staying Out of Trouble

There are plenty of opportunities for trouble to enter a teenager's life, whether at school, online, with friends, or even at home. Although many successfully avoid large doses of trouble, adolescence itself seems to breed it. In fact, some would argue that the adolescent brain's heightened need for stimulation acts as a kind of magnet for troubling behaviors, if not trouble itself. There to feed their already increased appetites for arousal are a complement of media-based agents offering a delectable array of models and examples specifically designed to seduce the adolescent, including but not limited to movies, the Internet, and even much of the unrated but no less provocative prime-time TV.

So how do we help our adolescents stay out of trouble? First of all, we recognize that we can no longer be their protectors. To succeed in that role requires total surrender to *our* control—which may make us feel better but is proven to stunt the growth of one of their most essential survival mechanisms, decision-making skills.

In fact, exceeding the recommended control limits for an adolescent often induces the opposite reaction from the one we seek: It can drive them *into* trouble. In adolescence at least, trouble often, but not always, begins at home and then quickly travels outward to other aspects of their lives. Just as we would never dream of offering them a cigarette, we shouldn't dream of inducing the fight-or-flight syndrome: We command; they resist; fight ensues; we overwhelm through force of threat; they retreat, often into the always welcoming clutches of trouble, or peers, or both. Each time we sever the connection, it's harder to get it back.

Alternatively, we use the Rules of Play as the starting (and ending) point for an ongoing conversation about trouble, its changing faces, its potential harms, how to avoid it, and what to do if they can't. We calmly point out how *no* can be their friend, and bad decisions their enemy. We set limits that our adolescents can understand and respect (thus accept), and establish that there will be consequences if or when they knowingly cross into unsafe territory.

III. Emotional and/or Psychological Safety

The intangibility of this third tier of the safety hierarchy makes it perhaps the most difficult to describe or prepare our adolescents for. It is also the trickiest because those whom our adolescents most trust can often cause the most damage. Whether through harassment or victimization by peers, subtle threats by other authority figures, or the pressures (both internal and external) to achieve and perform roles outside their normal ranges, adolescents are at heightened emotional and psychological risk. Already fearful of loneliness, adolescents often construct the very barriers that isolate them from their peers and loved ones. Then, once alone, they don't know how to make themselves heard and instead seek company in harmful thoughts that can lead to even more harmful actions. As our teenagers struggle under a tsunami of brain and body growth and development, our job is to talk them through it as best we can. We keep a careful watch for any abnormal patterns of behaviors or troubling conversations (see chapter 4, The Adolescent Mirror Distorts). Should we detect any, we must work quickly to restore any connections we might have severed with them. If the irregularities continue, we seek outside help.

So what do you mean by "Stay Safe"? they challenge.

Sensing a teachable moment, we reply, *First of all, stay clear of things that could get you hurt. The list is short* (emphasize this even if they think it's actually interminable—and don't forget the *whys*). And although adolescents often feel invulnerable in the face of other people's scary stories or statistics, it never hurts to reinforce a few key, albeit obvious, points:

1. Drunk Driving

Driving or riding with a driver who is under the influence, regardless of who it is, demonstrates a careless disregard not only for yourself but also for everyone else on the road. It is the worst kind of irresponsibility. In 2008, 12 percent of the 50,186 fatal car accidents involved drivers 15–20 years old. Every day, four teenagers die in car accidents involving alcohol.[3]

2. Drugs Can Cause Major and Undetected (Until Later) Damage to Your Brain and Body

For example, marijuana is a form of smoking, which we know damages lungs over time. Although not technically physically addictive, marijuana can be psychologically addictive by creating a dependency on its effects. As a matter of fact, marijuana is shown to affect alertness, concentration, and reaction time, among other skills. For example, a 2006 study reported that adolescents are more likely to drink and to smoke mari-juana once they can drive. The same study found similar acci-dent rates (38 percent versus 39 percent) among those who drove after drinking and after smoking marijuana.[4]

Solvents (such as glue) are highly toxic and addictive, and can actually lead to death by suffocation, heart failure, or choking on vomit. Solvents can also lead to headaches, nose-bleeds, and loss of smell or hearing.

Since 2008, use of harder drugs such as Ecstasy among adolescents has increased 67 percent. Marijuana use by teens has increased 22 percent. Perhaps the most alarming aspect of these findings is that the more normal drug and alcohol use becomes at younger ages, the less capable parents feel to cope with this new reality.[5]

According to a 2009 national survey, prescription drugs constitute the new kid on the adolescent-risk block, with close to 20 percent (4.7 million) able to access them for recreational purposes within an hour, one third (8.7 million) within a day.[6]

3. Drugs and the Law

Drugs and alcohol are illegal. (Remember number II, Staying Out of Trouble, on the *Stay Safe* hierarchy.) In most states, it is a crime for anyone under the legal drinking age of twenty-one to drink, possess, transport, buy, or even *try* to buy alcohol. Further, detecting liquor on an underage per-son's breath can lead to a charge of underage drinking. For minors in some states, police can and do use a prelimi-nary breath test (PBT), which is different from a regular Breathalyzer test and can lead to a conviction. It's also often illegal to carry a false ID, let alone use it to try to buy alcohol. If caught, in addition to a fine, teenagers can lose their right to drive for anywhere from ninety days to two years.

Be aware that many states are also cracking down on a social host law, which allows for a host to be sued by an injured party for furnishing alcohol to anyone under age twenty-one.

4. Sexually Transmitted Diseases

STDs can stay with you for life—as well as kill you (including HIV/ AIDS). New estimates on the number of newly diagnosed cases of STDs reveal that almost half of the 19 million cases diagnosed each year occur in fifteen- to twenty-four-year-olds, even though this age group represents only 25 percent of the overall population. In 2008, the two most common STDs were chlamydia and gonorrhea. Girls aged fifteen to nineteen reported the most cases.[7] Given these statistics, perhaps the most urgent conversations with our adolescents need to be about sex, particularly because fifteen- to seventeen-year-olds engage in oral sex and even intercourse as frequently in casual relationships as they do in more serious, committed ones.[8] (A different study found adolescents feel that oral sex is more consistent with their value systems, thus more acceptable.)[9]

Even though many adolescents don't consider oral sex to be sex, they can actually contract six different STDs from it.[10] Because their cervixes are covered with cells that are especially susceptible to STDs, adolescent girls represent the highest risk group. Up to one quarter of sexually active adolescent girls have been found to be infected with the HPV virus, many with a strain of the virus linked to cervical cancer.[11] There are several different strains of HPV, but the most common is genital warts. And unfortunately, the vast majority of HPVs, and most carriers, are not symptomatic.[12]

Chlamydia involves a bacterium that affects adolescent girls six times more frequently than adult women. Chlamydia can be transmitted via intercourse, oral sex, and even via eye fluids. Like HPV, chlamydia doesn't present symptoms. As a result, more than 75 percent of its victims don't even know they have it until they encounter difficulty getting pregnant, often years later.[13] Perhaps most alarmingly, a recent survey reported that adolescents between the ages of fifteen and seventeen find it easier to have sexual intercourse with a partner than to discuss the embarrassing topic of STDs.[14]

5. Pregnancy

Pregnancy is completely avoidable, and therefore irresponsible and unfair. Although teen pregnancy is at the lowest level ever recorded in the United States, research still shows that approximately three out of ten females get pregnant at least once before the age of twenty.[15] And, for the first time in fourteen years, teen pregnancy and birth rates are increasing.

> **US:** *So, how was the party? Were there a lot of kids going into the woods?*

If used effectively, and with luck, an innocuous additive embedded into a passing question can often jump-start a conversation. Sometimes this tactic backfires, but often it will not.

Using *going into the woods* as a euphemism for a spectrum of contraband and/or sexual activity, leapfrogs over the question of *whether* or *who,* leading us ever closer to *how much* and *what did you think about it*—which borders on, but doesn't cross over into, *were you?*

The objective of this phase of the conversation is to collect information as noninvasively as possible. The more nonchalant the collection process appears, the greater the chance that our adolescents will toss some crumbs of information in our direction, either to placate us or—and this is what we listen for—to signal any trouble. Any indication that we're using the information to build a case against them, or their friends or peers, will turn off the conversation faster than a blown fuse. So we tread carefully, always prepared to change the subject—quickly.

> **THEM:** *Sure. Kids go into the woods all the time. What do you think?*
> **US:** *Mostly to drink, or to smoke, too?*

Even-toned and nonjudgmental, we neither disapprove nor approve—yet. We just plot the dots to see if any kind of picture emerges.

> **THEM:** *Both. A few kids got pretty wasted.*
> **US:** *Did anyone pass out?*
> **THEM:** *No . . . not that I saw.*
> **US:** *What would you do if you saw someone pass out?*

We lob questions in their direction, hoping that our adolescents will field them.

> **US:** *You know that when someone passes out after drinking a lot, they could have alcohol poisoning and even die, right? Often kids are afraid, and even prevent others from getting help, for fear that they'll get in trouble. If you are ever in that situation, know that safety is always our main concern. In fact, we'd be proud of you for having the courage to put someone else's safety first.*

Notice that we can assert a very strong position on a solid basis without using a lot of *don't*s or threats: Our job is to keep them safe. It's about *protection,* not control or power. Whether offering alternative strategies or constantly reinforcing (or even subtly adjusting) the behavioral boundaries, we stick to the Rules of Play game plan.

But how do we find out if *they're* the ones drinking (or whatever)? Let's return to the earlier conversation:

> **THEM:** *Sure. Kids go into the woods all the time. But it's not like you have to go to be cool.*
> **US:** *Do they go mostly to drink, or to smoke, too?*
> **THEM:** *I don't know. I know what you're thinking. It was safe!*
> **US:** *What would happen, do you think, if kids were in the woods and the police or parents came?*
> **THEM:** *I don't know! Why are you asking me this?*

Knowing when a conversation is over as opposed to paused can be tricky. In general, when at all possible, we want to avoid hanging up first. Better to rest a few beats and see what happens. If they sense calm, they'll often jump back in, or we can.

> **THEM:** *They'd probably run away.*
> **US:** *Have you ever thought about what you would do if you were in that situation?*

Often our conversations with our adolescents are loaded with more than one potentially explosive issue. We try to manage this volatility by staying focused on one thing at a time—in this case, Staying Out of Trouble (number II in the *Stay Safe* hierarchy of safety issues). We do that by employing a *Here's what I'm worried about* approach to meting out our concerns.

THEM: *No, not really.*

US: *That would be pretty bad, wouldn't it? Whether you were involved or not, you could be reported to the school [many have rules that apply to outside-of-school activities] or arrested. Anything that ends up on your record could affect your driver's license or college acceptances or even future jobs. And there's nothing we or anyone but you can do about it. Better to think about these kinds of things ahead of time than to be caught unprepared.*

In the end, if the phone rings in the middle of the night, we don't want it to be the police or a hospital, we want it to be *them,* safe.

Rule #2: SHOW RESPECT

PERHAPS THE MOST IMPORTANT ROLE WE ASSUME AS PARENTS is that of a model to our children. And of all the qualities we attempt to model, showing respect may reap the biggest rewards, both for our adolescents and for us. Whether toward others or self, the respect that we demonstrate becomes the down payment on the respect that we ultimately earn from our adolescents. We start early with small displays such as listening without interrupting, acknowledging even the most trivial concern as real, and avoiding automatic assumptions that they are not really hurt or feeling sad, or that they are not telling the truth. By adolescence, we begin to see tangible evidence of them returning the favors.

Once we are certain that our teenagers have both witnessed and experienced the rewards and benefits of mutual and earned respect, we can insist on it as one of the three simple but unwavering Rules of Play.

We also know that adolescents cannot possibly anticipate the ways in which they will be tested—but we can. While they eagerly jump aboard many passing temptations and predilections, we try to foresee the hidden obstacles that they can't see. We strain to anticipate and evaluate the judgments they make when no one else is looking, weighing when and if to intercede. Modeling our best respect, we buttress their failures with clear consequences and a firm expectation that next time they will get it right.

US: *We can't know where you are and what you're doing every minute. But we do know that you're going to be making more and more decisions that will require making difficult choices.*

We even list some:

- Being in someone's home when there are no parents present.
- Whether to take drugs and/or drink alcohol.
- Whether to lie to get out of a situation.
- Driving with potentially unsafe or underage drivers.

US: *First and foremost, we want you to be safe, but we also need to feel comfortable that you're acting respectfully toward others, their property, and yourself.*

Again, this is *not* about control, it's about nourishing their decision-making muscles. It's about giving them enough room to make mistakes, while holding them accountable, even as we guide them. We need to know that they are safe, but neither can we rest easy unless we also know that they are acting honorably. And that applies to another's turf as well as their own (which also happens to be ours).

We also shouldn't hesitate to enhance our modeling with well-placed examples and stories. Since authenticity is less of an issue than impact, we embellish characters and incidents that stand the best chance of: (a) capturing their attention, and (b) delivering our message.

> **US:** *Did I ever tell you about the time that your aunt Karen came home to find that Ely had had a party without her permission and the house was trashed?*
> **THEM:** *No, what happened?*
> **US:** *You can imagine how upset Aunt Karen was. Probably the worst part was that she had always let Ely have friends over; kids seemed to gravitate to their house because he has such a great rec room. But when Ely, and kids she knew and trusted, let things get out of hand like that, she lost respect not only for Ely but for his friends, too. It took a long time for him to earn it back again. And it really changed Aunt Karen's view on things.*

We all need an Aunt Karen. Many trusted friends or relatives, preferably with some battle scars, will be happy to assume the role.

Storytelling allows us to present the situations and answer the questions our adolescents can't foresee. Used wisely, the well-placed story replaces a host of wasted words and unwelcome admonitions. Using our own, and their, malleable imaginations, we invent, resolve, and relive a multitude of potential worst cases. That way, should any of these scenarios become reality, our adolescents possess a supply of case examples that just might come in handy.

We treat respect like a rare gem, constantly marveling at its purity, proclaiming its virtues. Careful not to deface it, we neither take it for granted nor use it as a bargaining chip. Respect cannot be forced-fit or faked. We cannot give it unless we already own it, and if tarnished, it decreases in value. Like love, respect cannot be bought, and, if squandered, it is often harder to earn back, though it's never too late to try.

We expect nothing more and nothing less from this Rule of Play.

Rule #3: KEEP IN TOUCH

IT IS ACTUALLY OUR CHILDREN WHO TEACH US HOW TO PARENT. Yes, our own parents, perhaps a few books, and, if we're lucky, a good pediatrician or professional will provide useful advice for us to accept and reject. But we don't really learn the parenting craft without hands-on experience. And until we've parented an adolescent, we probably can't lay full claim to the wisdom that comes from this perspective.

As we struggle up the laborious, albeit spectacularly rewarding, parenting learning curve, our kids are also learning how to deal with *us*. In fact, research shows that by adolescence, they have already determined what kinds of information *we* have a right to know—and what we don't.[16] So it should come as no surprise that our teenagers are more forthcoming with information about their whereabouts and plans than about their own or their friends' individual relationships and activities. The stronger and more open our lines of communication, the more our adolescents will tell us. With just a few words, our adolescents can thwart our best intentions, create the sweetest harmony, or cause intolerable dissonance.

THEM: *I hate you. You never let me do anything. Why can't you be like other parents?*

Do they really hate us? No. Do these words indicate the onset of an insidious virus of disrespect? Not usually. Have they successfully severed a connection with sentiments like these? Only temporarily, hopefully. Will we experience a similar jolt to our parenting sensibilities each time our adolescents reveal their overloaded coping mechanisms this way? Very likely. In fact, we *want* our adolescents to use the best defense they've got, namely language, to protect themselves from a variety of psychological growing pains. As they learn to choose their words and control their impulses, we become an easy target for their practice.

US: *I'm sorry to make you so angry. We can talk more later when we both have given this some more thought.*

Then comes one of the hardest things for us *not* to do—lash back. Not wanting to be taken hostage by our own *Don't you dare talk to me like that* threats, we accept these tongue-lashings as signs of their need to back out of a corner or retreat. Rather than increase the heat on such volatile moments, we seek to dispel them with cooler heads and the healing power of time and space. Just enough.

Sometime later, we try:

US: *By the way, I've been thinking about the situation, and how about this as a compromise . . . ?*

And we start over, this time with a new game plan.

Once the lines of communication are open, staying in touch becomes a practical matter, a conduit through which good decisions are reinforced and bad ones weeded out. Masters at anticipating, we factor staying in touch down to a few simple variables. We need to know:

- When plans (and pre-anticipated contingencies) change.
- When the unanticipated arises and how they propose to deal with it.
- How they would respond in the face of danger.

US: *All we ask is that you let us know where you are and what you're up to, especially if plans change.*

Or, if they're not sure of their plans, choose a designated time or specific circumstances under which they must check in.

US: *That will give us the peace of mind we need to know that you are safe.*
THEM: *So what you're saying is that if we decide to go get a pizza, then go back to Kyle's house instead of Randy's where I originally thought I'd be, I have to call or text you twice in the space of an hour? Do you see how ridiculous that is?*
US: *That does sound like a bit much, doesn't it? Let's see, it's six-thirty now, why don't you check in at nine o'clock and let me know what you're up to, and we'll take it from there.*

Not only does staying in touch trigger the *no-questions-asked* deal (*no matter what is going on, we'll come and get you— no questions asked*), but it also stakes out our position as "home base." Never before has keeping in touch been so easy; but never has it been so easy for our adolescents to avoid the truth. Both of these realities underscore the importance of keeping the conversation with our adolescents ongoing.

And when the strains of resistance inevitably creep in (the refrain often including words like *no one else's parents make them do this* or *why can't you just trust me*), we're always prepared with a rebuttal or three. We need only gently remind them that there are really only three things being asked of them, which is many fewer than most parents' rules . . . and surely they don't want us to lose sleep at night.

Working together with our adolescents, we pave our connection with three simple but concrete Rules of Play. We also willingly step aside as they barrel by us in pursuit of one adolescent goal or another. While we expect to know where they're going, we don't insist on tagging along or trailing them.

> **US:** *I'm glad you called about the change in plans, but we never discussed your spending the night at an entirely different house.*
> **THEM:** *But plans changed, and she's already having two people, so her mom said it was fine to have two more. C'mon, it's going to be really fun and these kids never include me. This is a big deal!*
> **US:** *You know I'm not good with last-minute surprises. Here's what I need to know . . .*

Then fill in the blank with a *reasonable* request for enough details to prove that the three Rules of Play are at work—say, a call from a parent (or a way for you to reach them), further details regarding transportation and who else is involved, or the like.

US: *Call me back when you have that information and we'll take it from there. How much time do you think you need to do that?*

THEM: *Why are you doing this? Nobody else's parents make them do this stuff!*

US: *I'm sorry if it seems like a lot. But we were fine with Plan A, and we'll probably be fine with this new plan. I'm only asking for three things. You know if you spring something like this without enough details, the answer is usually an automatic no. So it's up to you to make it work. I'll be standing by for your text at [designated time]. If I don't hear from you by then, I'll assume we're back to Plan A, and I'll see you at home at eleven o'clock [or whatever]. And we can talk this all through later in case there's a next time. Okay?*

No anger, no raised voices, no room for further discussion or negotiation. We lean on the three Rules of Play to guide, support, and lend a helping reason. In the event of a breach of faith or trust, we remind them that a broken Rule of Play necessitates a reevaluation of at least their plans, if not a lot more, to regain any lost ground. As with any guidelines, the Rules of Play will succeed only if both sides—teenagers and parents—stick to them. Think of the Rules of Play as the double-sided tape that binds us to our adolescents.

Although it may sound as if we are preaching a laissez-faire approach, that is not our intention. We all know that parenting is not just a job; rather, we wear it like a second skin, a skin we cannot shed. It glows with pride and reveals bruises and scratches. The real intention of this book is to help ease the growing pains—theirs and ours—that inevitably accompany adolescence.

Maybe for our own peace of mind, or to mollify that sinking feeling that there are things now that they don't want us to know, we ask our adolescents to humor us by repeating the Rules of Play aloud, like a mantra—or a prayer—each time they head out the door, into the far-flung and unstable reaches of adolescence. Stay safe, show respect, keep in touch.

PART II

The Seven Things

THEIR BRAINS
ARE TO BLAME

WE HAVE ALL WITNESSED THE RAPID, UNPREDICTABLE SHIFTS IN our adolescents' demeanors. Adolescents don and shed moods as nonchalantly as gym clothes, leaving us to sort the discards. New research on the adolescent brain suggests that many of the behavioral vicissitudes we observe in today's adolescent may have physiological roots. Hormones no longer suffice as a simple explanation for a complex set of brain chemistry–induced teenage behaviors. Granted, sex hormones do run rampant in the adolescent bloodstream, and a favorite landing place is the brain's limbic system. But these hormones are more coconspirators than lone culprits in what seems like a mind and body under teenage siege. Indeed, new brain research provides a welcome opportunity to reexamine our adolescents from the perspective of a brain undergoing a major growth surge. Suddenly their struggles to make sense out of a vast array of contending influences—ranging from us, to peers, the media, the Internet, and widespread accessibility to alcohol, drugs, and sexual material—have a new context.

Though we may not be able to relate to many of our

adolescents' current experiences, we can all relate to the feeling of being overwhelmed.

More News About the Adolescent Brain

WHILE THE SIGNPOSTS OF ADOLESCENCE, SUCH AS MOODINESS, fatigue, and impulsivity point to universally recognizable behaviors, their root causes, until recently, have been couched in developmental psycho-speak and/or passed off as the result of some combination of hormones, bad parenting, or even bad luck. Therefore, it is always reassuring when plaguing, discomfiting symptoms reveal physiological roots.

Most of us are usually aware when a scientific finding is deemed potentially appetizing to the general public. A rash of news articles sprinkle just enough information to titillate but not satisfy our desire to make use of a featured event or discovery. The fact that about 95 percent of a child's brain growth occurs by age five is no longer headline worthy, but the growth antics of the remaining 5 percent during adolescence is.[1]

Following is a parenting primer (which means "only what we need to know—and nothing more") on the wiring (both hard and soft) of the adolescent brain.

Think of the adolescent brain as a brand-new airport. The construction of the runways, terminals, and infrastructure is all completed by year five, but the wiring and programming necessary to enable the control tower to function efficiently and safely won't be completed until around age twenty, despite steadily increasing demands on it. Now imagine the frustration of the airport pilots (that is, our adolescents) who are convinced of their readiness to fly solo, but are constantly prevented from doing so by a variety of authorities. No wonder they convey their impatience by perpetually revving their engines (usually in our faces), unaware and unconcerned about the dangers that await them. Who needs a fully functioning control tower, anyway?

THE ADOLESCENT BRAIN'S CONTROL MECHANISMS

FROM BIRTH, OUR BRAINS ARE READY TO ATTEND TO OUR basic survival requirements. These primitive needs—hunger satisfaction, pain sensitivity, fight or flight, sexual drive—continue, to this day, to be under the management of a powerful region called the *limbic system,* also known as the emotional brain. But the limbic system is helpless when it comes to dealing with our more civilized, or human, capacities such as conflict resolution, decision making, planning, organizing, and impulse inhibition. These occur in the "higher" regions of the brain (the control tower) that don't fully develop until around the midtwenties. This region, called the *prefrontal cortex,* operates from its front-and-center location, right behind the forehead. Equipped to override the more primal needs of the limbic system, the prefrontal cortex controls such impulses as when to act on anger, succumb to temptation, and seek immediate gratification. In other words, the prefrontal cortex is the seat of our judgment.

Now think of adolescence as the manifestation of an intense rivalry between the pleasure-seeking limbic system and control-central, the prefrontal cortex, both of which are undergoing major development. The struggle for domination between these two parts of the brain thrusts our adolescents into a seemingly suspended state of unrest, like a cerebral junkie in constant search of the next stimulating fix. As parents, we observe this struggle from a close proximity that, on occasion, makes us a target for some sharp-edged attitudes and frustrations.

Fortunately, as the growth spurt accelerator eases up, so does the intensity of the limbic system–prefrontal cortex rivalry, so that by early adulthood the two areas learn to coexist in a healthy competition, each with its own strengths and weaknesses. Lest we feel entirely helpless during this protracted brain-development process (that is, adolescence), there are things we can do to help our teenagers through it, thus also helping ourselves. But that requires a little further analysis of the rivalry itself.

What We Need to Know About the Limbic System

PICTURE THE ADOLESCENT LIMBIC SYSTEM AS A BUNCH OF EXposed nerves. Like a bared tooth root, these nerves are highly sensitive to even the slightest sensation, let alone the bombardment they actually receive on a daily basis. Now add enormous waves of new cell growth, including sex hormones, to this area and we begin to understand why the raw emotions indigenous to the limbic system—anger, aggression, fear, elation, and/or sadness—might appear out of control, particularly when an adolescent must choose among multiple options or alternatives. This may help to clarify our adolescents' inability to decipher between such clear (to us) concepts as right versus wrong, friend versus foe, danger versus safety.

> **US:** *Why was your sister screaming downstairs?*
> **THEM:** *It's fine now. I just scared her a little.*
> **US:** *No kidding! What did you do?* [Even-toned, no emotional labels showing.]

THEM: *I lit a match near that new coat she's so addicted to. All I wanted to do was borrow it, but no way, not her precious little possession.*

If the voice wasn't so matter-of-fact, or coming from an adolescent, we might assume this to be some kind of joke.

US: *You lit a match and held it up to her jacket?*
[Struggling now to stay calm.]
THEM: *Don't worry, she wasn't wearing it. It was on the counter. Anyway, everything's fine. Nothing happened.*

No, it isn't fine, and yes, this warrants immediate consequences, but the point here is to reveal the invisible fault lines that undermine the reasoning skills of the adolescent.

What We Need to Know About the Prefrontal Cortex

MEANWHILE, THE PREFRONTAL CORTEX, EAGER TO RESTRAIN the volatile limbic system, lays down a series of inhibitory connections between these two parts of the brain. These connections not only ward off the wayward impulses coming from the limbic system, but also supply such critical reasoning tools as the ability to plan and anticipate, and, perhaps most important, the ability to reflect on a decision. Over time and with use, these tools enable the safe delivery of consistently reliable judgments. But like any major development project, this brain-centered construction site is subject to continuous disruption, including intermittent blasts, constant detours, and general disarray.

As the seat of judgment, the prefrontal cortex has another

critical mission: to sponsor the evolution of our adolescents' abstract reasoning skills, otherwise known as a license to question ... everything, including us. We welcome this new intellectual companion like we welcome their drivers' licenses, with mixed emotions ranging from liberation and pride to dread. Heady from the daily discoveries associated with the newfound powers of abstraction, our adolescents launch an all-out search for their bounds, hoping not to find any.

As our adolescents expand their capacity to think abstractly, we begin to notice how small decisions open into bigger ones: Kids gathering at a friend's house becomes a party; innocent friendships become relationships; and appetites are more than a quest to satisfy hunger or thirst. They flaunt their ability to explore the many sides of an issue with alarming alacrity. With each question or explanation, their resistance muscles seem to gain in strength. We notice the constant repositioning of many of our carefully placed stakes in the ground. Meanwhile, slightly intoxicated by the elevated level of conversation with our adolescents, we are lulled into fantasies of a serene and distant land called (their) adulthood—just around the bend.

THE GREAT BRAIN DRAIN

THE ADOLESCENT BRAIN-GROWTH SPURT IS PERHAPS BEST viewed as a massive-overproduction-followed-by-pruning process during which only those cells that are used survive (not unlike the fertilization process). In other words, a straight *use-it-or-lose-it* proposition. While this second wave of overproduction peaks just as the puberty front rolls in, it is the ongoing pruning process that defines the neural pathways and brain functionality that will endure long after the adolescent development storm has subsided. Just as the cutting back of a tree or plant allows the surviving parts to flourish, it is the cutting back, or shedding, of unused brain cells and pathways that allows the vibrant parts of the brain to grow and burgeon. Although much of this process occurs naturally, we can, in fact, help determine which cells get used—and which get lost. *Control it? no; help to influence their brain development? yes.*

During the first growth spurt, spanning years one through five, we (often unwittingly) managed the pruning process by placing our children in a perpetual state of stimulation, mostly to keep them busy and us sane. Our little ones happily obliged, allowing their brains to stretch and shed with abandon. During this second spurt, not only have we been deposed from our top management positions, but we also confront rivals we never dreamed possible, from the Internet and peers of often unknown origin and/or unproven credentials, to substances that threaten permanent damage to this new crop of yet-unprotected brain cells. Now it is our adolescents, not us, who control how their brain power gets allocated. This time around, we must settle for the role of influencer. And influence we can. Not by trying to control everything that their brain does and doesn't do, but by steering them in the right directions.

Despite many impressive attempts by our teenagers to outsmart us, we still possess two key advantages. One, we have enough perspective to know that, as with pregnancy, the outcome is inevitable: They will grow up, because of us—and despite us. We also know that not one, but myriad paths will lead them to the inevitable destination of adulthood. The second advantage we possess is the ability to discern the difference between the easiest path and the best path to take.

By choosing paths of least resistance, our adolescents can bypass opportunities to expand new areas of their brains. For example, those who choose to spend their time more passively, watching television or idly listening to music, inadvertently donate those unused synapses to the pruning process. On the other hand, adolescents who pursue a musical instrument, sports, or other active, brain-stimulating activities stabilize and strengthen many different neural connections and pathways, all vital to learning. This is how the *use-it-or-lose-it* proposition plays out in the adolescent brain. The simple, repetitive use of a particular neural path ensures its survival. The unused paths (and passive activities qualify as nonuse) gradually disappear. The surviving neural networks and connections then get myelinated, or wrapped in a Saran Wrap–like substance, to ensure their longevity. The stronger the neural networks, the stronger the sheathing, or insulation. The stronger the insulation, the better the conductivity, and the more capable our adolescents become.

The brain constantly takes cues from its environment, literally consuming whatever it is fed. If it's plied with violent images or other aberrations, the naïve adolescent brain (specifically the amygdala, a tiny part of the limbic system) will interpret those behaviors as normal and imprint them for future use. The heightened impressionability of the adolescent brain, coupled with an inability to discriminate among the nuances of strong emotions, creates the breeding ground for violence to beget violence and mistakes to repeat themselves.

SUBSTANCE ABUSE AND THE ADOLESCENT BRAIN

EVEN MORE ALARMING ARE THE EFFECTS OF DRUGS (INCLUDing nicotine and alcohol) on the developing brain. Although much of this research has been confined to rats (for obvious reasons), the findings have wide implications for our adolescents.

One study on the effects of alcohol on the brain found more brain damage in adolescent rats than adult ones, particularly in the area associated with addiction and memory. Specifically, alcohol use disrupted the development of the hippocampus, the part of the brain associated with long-term memory development, causing it to actually decrease in size. Because rats and humans share a similar neurobiology underlying memory formation, this study concluded that alcohol poses real long-term danger to the adolescent brain.[2] Alcohol also disturbs the developing cerebellum, the part of the brain that controls not only coordination but other complex behaviors. Alcohol does not seem to sedate or impair gross motor coordination in adolescents to the extent that it does in adults. Therefore, adolescents may possess a false sense of control when it comes to driving under the influence or other risky behaviors. Riding high from dopamine surges that ambush critical inhibitory signals and elevate moods, adolescents may be inclined to imbibe larger amounts, increasing dependency and the tendency to binge. This rapid ingestion of alcohol into the brain can actually shut down the hippocampus, causing blackouts. The adolescent brain is much more sensitive to attack on this memory center.

A different study found that the adolescent brain also responds more intensely to nicotine than does the brain of adults, causing permanent behavior problems, most noticeably in girls. After two weeks of receiving nicotine injections, not only did the adolescent female rats show increased nicotine receptors (a sign of addiction), but they were more lethargic as well. In addition, female brains had decreased production of two chemicals known to be lower in depressed people: dopamine and norepinephrine.[3] Yet another study of teens who smoked 12–14 cigarettes a day found impaired verbal working memories (critical for paragraph comprehension). The earlier they had started, the worse the impairment. This was particularly true in boys who tend to start smoking at younger ages.[4]

Stronger, more nimble than ours, the adolescent brain learns faster (including what feels good), making them more vulnerable to drug use and stronger addictions. So once they start, not only is it harder to quit, they are more susceptible to relapse.[5]

So the next time we witness our adolescents under the influence of an errant mood or decision, we might remind ourselves that somewhere within the recesses of their brains a battle is being waged between the limbic system and the prefrontal cortex. Rather than inserting ourselves into the middle of the conflict, we let the more impartial Rules of Play arbitrate. By constantly reinforcing the Rules of Play as their guide, we help our adolescents solidify the neural pathways that we know will lead them in the right direction.

SLEEP AND THE ADOLESCENT BRAIN

UNLIKE OUR BODIES, OUR BRAINS POWER UP RATHER THAN down during coveted slumbering hours. Like elves in Santa's workshop, the brain sets about such essential chores as replaying the day's learning, coding, storing, and shooing worthy items from the short-term to the long-term memory (hippocampus). During sleep, concepts take shape, connections get reinforced. Conductivity improves, defense systems fortify. Think of sleep as one of the brain's most important vitamins.

Unlike us, adolescents secrete melatonin, the hormone that induces sleep, from eleven P.M. until eight A.M., making that the optimal time frame for them to sleep.[6] (For those of us who haven't noticed the onset of mid-evening drowsiness, our secretions begin earlier.) Therefore, forcing adolescents to go to bed earlier or wake up earlier not only is futile, but also deprives them of much-needed sleep, and leads to reactions as mild as irritability and as severe as depression. Lack of sleep has also been linked to an increase in the number of car accidents and cases of ADHD.[7]

In fact, the repercussions of overtiredness are spreading. One study reported that overtired three-to-eight-year-olds were almost three times as likely to binge drink at ages eighteen to twenty.[8] Since 84 percent of teens report sleeping with their cell phones (both for its use as a clock/alarm as well as to text), we might add the benefits of sleep vs. connectivity to the Stay Safe list in the Rules of Play.[9]

Sleep experts from Columbia to Stanford universities also agree that most adolescents do not get the nine-plus hours per night needed, and those getting less than five hours per night are 71 percent more likely to suffer from anxiety disorders and even depression.

Adolescents who live with an earlier rather than later lights-out policy *do* get more sleep, and the benefits *do* show.[10]

Interestingly, a poll of three thousand high school students in Rhode Island showed that adolescents who received more than eight hours of sleep per night scored higher grades than those who received less.[11]

STRESS AND THE ADOLESCENT BRAIN

ANOTHER NASCENT AREA OF ADOLESCENT BRAIN RESEARCH surrounds the effects of stress. Psychologists' offices have long been populated by patients suffering from such chronic disorders as depression and anxiety. However, more recently, adolescent mental health providers report a significant uptick in anxiety-like symptoms as adolescents struggle to juggle more harder and faster.

An audible collective sigh of relief could be heard throughout the parenting community with the news that those who had neglected to immerse their newborns in Baby Einstein at birth had not deprived them of reading rights by age four. And those of us awed by an early-reading child can curtail any fantasies of guaranteed acceptance to the college of choice. In fact, the more we learn about brain development, the more many things stay the same. For instance, we can no more rush the brain to develop than we can force adolescents to grow taller, be motivated, or believe that they are the best at something because we say so. The more they feel forced, rushed, prodded before they're ready, the more the brain has to respond the only way it knows how: by calling up its own protective reinforcements. In too many cases, that reinforcement is a hormone called cortisol. Like a skunk releasing its self-preserving scent, cortisol triggers its own form of protection. This powerful chemical thrusts the brain into its fight-or-flight stance, stifling assistance from the deliberative reasoning sponsorship of the prefrontal cortex.

Once the immediate threat (or pressure to perform) resolves, the cortisol naturally subsides (although *much* more slowly in the adolescent brain than in the adult one); the prefrontal cortex relaxes, and brain life returns to normal. Quick hits, small doses, fast acting: a wonder hormone? Not so, we're finding in the high-expectation, high-threat world of the assumed-to-be-high-functioning adolescent.

Once again, rats are our friends when it comes to teaching us about the adolescent brain. Whether it's the increase in anxiety-like symptoms (difficulty sleeping, eating, concentrating) among adolescents that is driving new brain research, or whether the research itself is heightening our awareness of these developmental disruptions, is unclear. What is clear is that *any* traceable amount of corticosterone (the rodent version of cortisol) in a pubescent rat reveals noticeable depressive symptoms during adulthood, ratifying the belief that constant stress during adolescence raises the likelihood of mood-related disorders later on. The ill effects of stress have been found in the adolescent hippocampus and the central nervous system. Like an army ready for battle, stress stands up the prefrontal cortex in a suspended state of arousal. This unnatural state eventually leads to alterations in the pubertal nervous system.[12]

In essence, stress restructures the development of the adolescent brain. Such structural remodeling diminishes the efficiency of the adolescent working memory (the hippocampus), making it harder for them to concentrate. In an ironic twist of brain functionality, stress adds to stress by creating a catch-22 in which our adolescents actually feel as if they're working harder yet are actually accomplishing less. They're tired, want to sleep, but can't. Sleep, the vehicle that allows the brain to do its heaviest hauling, transferring new learning from short- to long-term memory, gets interrupted.

The adolescent brain, at the height of its final growth spurt, learns faster, better, stronger than it ever will again. That is, under the right circumstances—high challenge, low threat—the adolescent brain busily constructs connective pathways with the might of a neural army. Under stressful conditions—high challenge—*high* threat—the adolescent brain actually loses efficiency. The little engine that couldn't. Just as hunger pangs trigger a desire for food, stress too seeks its own relief. Too often, relief comes in the form of high risks, like binging, cutting—or worse. That almost one-half of teens (45 percent) don't recognize the risk of underage drinking may indicate a new normal in a day in the life of an adolescent.[13]

TECHNOLOGY AND THE ADOLESCENT BRAIN

JUST AS THE HUMAN BODY CHANGES IN RESPONSE TO FOOD IN-take, MRI evidence confirms that our brains are also reshaping in response to the many hours per day focused on the screens in our lives. Few of us bat an eyelash at the many Kaiser Foundation–like studies that validate what we already know: Our adolescents are like digital rats who forage through online alleys in search of enlightenment—as much as 8.5 hours a day (see chapter 5, Friends Don't Matter As Much as We May Think). A baseline study found that after just five hours on the Internet, subjects' brains had rewired, particularly in the control tower—the prefrontal cortex.[14] Since we already know that repeated behaviors imprint themselves on the brain, the bigger question is, How does this alter the conversation with our adolescents?

> **US:** *Humor me. Tell me all the reasons why you like social networking/videogames.*
> **THEM:** (girl): *Okayyy. I like that I can see what's going on with different friends and that I can stay in touch with friends that don't live nearby, like camp kids. I can even make new ones . . .*
> Or:
> **THEM:** (boy): *Okayyy. They're fun and challenge me. I get to play against lots of different people . . .*
> Then:
> **US:** *I get it [*even if you don't, try a spoonful of sugar to help it go down*]. Can you guess what worries me about so much time online? [*See whether, once again, their savvy surprises, then continue.*]*
> *Three things [*you may want to pick one or two, then look for another opening later, remembering that

once is not usually enough when it comes to brain training].

1. I've learned recently that even though it feels like it can, our brains can't actually do more than one thing at a time. It actually takes time for your brain to shift back and forth from one thing to another.

2. If you're on late at night, the blue light from the computer screen can actually fool your brain into thinking you're not tired, [the more technical explanation involves how that blue light affects a protein in the eye called cryptochrome which controls our body clocks by suppressing melatonin release*]*.

3. Computer play usually doesn't involve—and often replaces—deep reading, which affects everything from how you think to how you speak and come across to others.

A conversation need only start to make a point.

Technology is like a drug to the adolescent who mainlines instant gratification. In fact, technology-stimulated brains also produce that friendly feel-good brain chemical, dopamine, that alcohol ingestion does, leaving them wanting more. They flip through websites like magazine pages, inhaling headlines, images, news flashes, homework help into their highly receptive brains. But until and unless that information sorts itself into meaningful, usable piles, the result of a successful transfer from the short- to the long-term memory, it goes the way of most prefinal exam cramming.

Information doesn't make us smarter, knowledge does. Instantaneous servings of bite-sized facts, social candy, and entertainment tidbits train the adolescent brain to crave these morsels of short-term gratification. But until that information formulates a reason, leads to a deduction, draws an inference, it will not grow them smarter.

Smarter happens when adolescents use new information to take on a different point of view, and apply it to something going on in the world, or when they contribute to a discussion in the classroom, at the dinner table, among curious, challenging friends. But when released from the obligation to interpret, the brain skips a critical stepping stone to complex thinking. Just as reading is a learned skill, so too is thinking, and the deeper the thought process, the better on both counts.

Only when information makes its way from the short-term storage of the working memory to the categorized warehouse of the longer-term one are we able to access and apply it to myriad situations. Only then does information flower into knowledge.

Adolescents bore easily, complain about lengthy reading assignments, chafe quickly when hands and minds are bound to a single activity—all evidence of neural network calibration. The very creators of the information gluttony, the software industry, have coined a phrase to describe the adolescent addiction to multitasking: *continuous partial attention.* Teachers describe its symptoms in terms of shortened attention spans, the inability to delay gratification, to stay focused, read longer articles or books effectively, absorb complexity. Efficiency over immediacy, as one psychologist calls it.[15] University researchers find that students rarely return to the original site of their search to dig more deeply, typically reading only one to two pages on any one site.

Despite the fact that the brain processes billions of signals per second, fielding and filing faster than the speed of light, and despite the constant barrage of "apps," inputs and information, this we now know from the world of brain research: The brain is *incapable* of doing more than one task simultaneously. Rather, the brain must shift and refocus *each and every time* we ask it to transfer our attention. Miraculously, the brain accomplishes this elaborate do-si-do deftly and obediently.

Unfortunately, it does so at varying speeds, based on a host of factors ranging from age to familiarity. More often than we care to recognize, productivity and efficiency take its toll.

So, before we correlate too many hours spent "doing" homework with heavy-handed work assignments, we might factor in the multiple inputs that may be impeding the completion process.

Whether to settle a debate over who invented what, or when or where to find the best deal on air filters, we are our own empirical data that substantiates that we don't need to read an entire book, or even article, to *sound* knowledgeable. Nevertheless, *our* brain training was undeniably different than that of our adolescents'. Rather than firehosed with information, we had to excavate for it, intuit our way to conclusions, usually following single, sequential paths. So abundant and myriad are the paths and sources of information available to our adolescents that they almost have to defend themselves from the onslaughts. As a result, they skim more than they deep dive, deselect rather than closely examine. This is the brain training *they* need to survive and thrive in a world of much broader and diverse demands and perspectives.

Put simply, their brains encode differently than ours, and need to in order to survive their futures. We can no more deprive them of the tools they need to develop their version of survival skills than our parents could have deprived us of the desire to push their boundaries of success. The difference is that most of our adolescents need only go as far as their rooms to find an amusement park full of "uni-tainment" options, or whole university libraries full of information. Unfortunately, these types of pseudo interactions actually inhibit the development of pathways in the brain devoted to honing critical thinking and essential interpersonal and empathic skills sorely needed in the twenty-first century.

Japan has provided some of the most interesting research regarding the effects of excessive use of technology on the brain. One such finding demonstrates that playing video games actually suppresses activity in the prefrontal cortex, activating instead the part of the brain that controls vision and movement. When the same subjects performed a simple math problem, however, a much broader area of the brain pitched in, including parts that control memory and even impulse control (the limbic system), shedding new light on the benefits (or lack thereof) of video game usage.[16]

As the adolescent brain busily fields a constant barrage of inputs, psychologists bear witness to a resulting psychological dyspepsia, sometimes compared to the grogginess that clouds our brains after too much TV or a long movie. The resulting brain indigestion leaves our adolescents stuffed but unsatisfied. To cope with the stress of this discomfort, their brains instinctively call out the cortisol troops to numb things down. And the cycle begins again(see previous section on Stress and the Adolescent Brain).

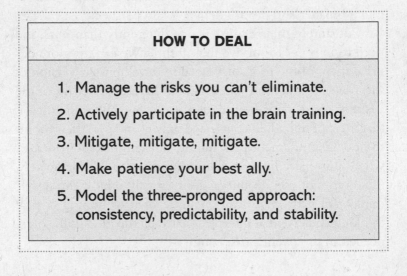

HOW TO DEAL

1. Manage the risks you can't eliminate.

2. Actively participate in the brain training.

3. Mitigate, mitigate, mitigate.

4. Make patience your best ally.

5. Model the three-pronged approach: consistency, predictability, and stability.

1. Manage the Risks You Can't Eliminate

Perhaps the most insidious aspect of the surging adolescent brain is its ability to lure us into actually believing that a lesson has been learned, a danger understood, a promise kept—despite a trail of evidence to the contrary. At times, our adolescents' level of con artistry qualifies them for the CIA—or the Mafia.

> **THEM:** *Everybody's going! You said I could go if there was a group going! Well, there is.*
>
> **US:** *You're right, I did say that. But I also said that since none of you had been there before, you either needed adult supervision or you had to be with someone who knows her way around. Just give me a plan for how the whole thing will work, and we can discuss it.*
>
> **THEM:** *What is this, a business? I told you who was going and how we're getting there. What's the big deal? Stop doubting me. Lots of kids go there—all the time. It's perfectly safe.*
>
> **US:** *I'm sure it is. I'm just worried about the risks involved with going to a strange place where you could easily get separated or lost. I'm not saying no right now, I'm just asking for a plan that shows me how you're going to stay safe and in touch.*

Certified custodians of their safety, we listen as they plead their case—and that of their peers—and then fill in the blanks left by a still-developing prefrontal cortex. Avoiding the *no* land mines guaranteed to cause an explosion, we focus on the plans:

- *This is what I need to be able to rule in your favor.*
- *Provide it and you're in business.*

Making plans to an adolescent can be as much an anathema as paying taxes is to us. (Maybe we're both hoping for some unforeseen means to materialize.) To assist, we offer suggestions: *Tell me what you've tried?* or *Would you like to know what others have done in this situation?* or *Do you have any other options?*

Because adolescents are not conditioned, or even able, to see the gray areas, their requests and wishes tend to come in only two colors: black or white. They set their sights on the results they seek and assume that sheer force of desire will protect them from any unanticipated dangers. Knowing that reasoned judgments (at least consistently) are simply beyond their capability, we lead them through the dance steps needed to learn good decision making. What feels awkward and clumsy at first becomes, with enough repetition and practice, rote and reflexive. Eventually, they even stop stepping on our toes.

2. Actively Participate in the Brain Training

Reacting to brain-induced cravings for new sources of sustenance and stimulation, healthy or not, safe or not, our adolescents constantly and unconsciously snack on the latest media, Internet, fashion, and sports trends. Rather than quenching their appetites, many of these artificially flavored enticements only intensify their cravings. Often and inexplicably, we find them in the trancelike grip of such brain-contracting influences as incendiary rap music or reality-contorting TV. Sometimes, we wrench them free in the hope of preserving future brain cells. Other times, we have no choice but to wait for their reemergence from this self-inflicted isolation.

> **THEM:** *Okay, okay, this is almost over; I'll finish then. I promise.*

US: *But you've been playing that video game for two hours! I need you to finish right now.*

Long pause during which what was already obvious becomes more so: They did not hear us because they do not want to. But they meet our half step toward a more desperate measure with:

THEM: *C'mon, I said I would be right there! I've been working hard. Just give me a little break, will you?*
US: *Sure. For how long?*

We let them respond because we understand that their brains run at a different clock speed from ours. If we agree with the compromise, we set a mental timer (because they won't) and hold them to it. If we don't agree, we adjust accordingly:

US: *And what happens if you don't?*

Again we let our adolescents respond while assuming the burden of holding them accountable—that is, if we want to actively train their brains. If we forget, or abdicate, then we should expect this scene, or one like it, to replay itself over and over. (And it might anyway, depending on the age and stage of the adolescent. But at least we've created a drill for them to expect—and practice.)

Sometime later, preferably out of range of physical escape hatches—maybe in the car:

US: *Guess what I read? [*Remember, no response doesn't necessarily mean that they're not listening.*] Want to hear? It might shock you.*

THEM: *What?*

US: *What you put in your brain right now, while you're a teenager, has a big effect on how smart you will be for the rest of your life.* [No, that wasn't very clear, but we're still vying for their attention.]

THEM: *What are you talking about?*

Got it!—if only for a few more seconds. Never underestimate the power of the "There you go making no sense again" attention–getting device, which is akin to the ever-popular "I'm not afraid to make a fool of myself."

US: *Two things: Did you know that your brain is going through its biggest and final growth spurt, right now, until you're about twenty? This article compared your brain to a big construction site that's in the process of building all sorts of connections, like pathways and bridges, between all its different functions like memory and reasoning and organization. The connections being built right now are the ones that will last your whole life. Except those you don't use, die off—forever!* [Pause, take a breath.]

Guess what part of your brain is most damaged by drugs and alcohol? [These words usually get their attention, so treat the question rhetorically.] *Your memory and your judgment. Also, any brain cells that you kill by using alcohol or drugs die forever.* [And, in case they didn't hear, or get, it the first time . . .] *They don't come back.*

THEM: *Then you don't have anything to worry about cuz I use my brain all the time.*

US: *Yep, I see that. But what's scary is the fact that if you don't use it, you lose it! According to this article, things like watching videos or looking at pictures or chatting online*

*don't count as using your brain and actually cause brain
cells to die off, like dead skin.*
THEM: *That's ridiculous. I use my brain when I'm
online!*
US: *Not really; that's considered too passive. That kind of
sedentary activity actually allows brain cells to slough off.*
THEM: *Oh, I see what this is about.*

Even if they don't say any of this, there's a very good
chance they're thinking it.

US: *The opposite is true, too. The more connections you
make, the deeper you think, the better your brain will
function—your whole life.*
THEM: *So how do I make these connections?*
US: *Through all the good stuff you do—reading, sports,
playing the guitar [or whatever]* . . .

While we can't affect the pace and progress of the growth
and development going on in our adolescents' brains, we can
assist in the conditioning by orchestrating exposure to different types of experiences, pleasures, and activities. Think about
it this way: There before us sits a surprisingly clean slate.
Though it is not ours to fill in, we can supply the markers—
as well as some inspiration. Our adolescents might be imper-
vious to such threats and warnings as dying cells and memory
damage, but we are not. So we try to post them in ways and
places that our adolescents are most likely to notice.

We might be consoled to know that the real adversary in
our adolescents' lives is not us, or their peers, or even the evil
media empire. Our adolescents' most ardent adversaries lie
within. And while they can't see the internal agitation, they
can certainly sense its presence each time a pleasure-seeking

limbic system tries to prevail over a more judicious prefrontal cortex. Though stuck on the outside, that does not diminish our role or our ability to help our adolescents resolve these internal conflicts. Ultimately, the most potent deterrent or influence regarding whether *to do or not to do, go or not to go* revolves around the continued and consistent imprint of only three immutable requirements: the Rules of Play—stay safe, show respect, keep in touch.

3. Mitigate, Mitigate, Mitigate

Where does the unwelcome brain interloper, stress, come from, inquiring parental minds want to know. Like so many complex questions, the answers follow suit. Few kids today are exempt from the pressure to perform; maybe not on every stage or even on a public stage, but school, social contexts, church, playing fields, all require performance. For some, stress drivers nag from within with no apparent provocation. Others obsess over the need to please or earn approval. Athletes, in particular, suffer from fear of nonperformance.

The parenting job description contains more duties and skills than a large-scale rescue operation: manager, nurse, resident expert, negotiator, magician, prognosticator, maintenance crew, tutor, banker, the list goes on. On demand. But one role we should not add to the list, regardless of our own needs or projections, is that of stress inducer.

If anxiety is fear gone wild, then stress is fear of disappointment gone wilder. Not the big disappointments, like cheating or a major Rule of Play infraction; those warrant a strong show of disappointment. But the nagging, relentless drone of unmet expectations that play like a pitchfork on a blackboard to the finely attuned adolescent. *Why did you . . . ?* sounds a lot like, *You're not quite good enough. Why can't you just . . . ?* sounds like a cacophonous *Why do you think I work so hard to provide for you?* Even the old reliable *We just want you to do your best* can shift the desire to achieve from its rightful owner, themselves, to the other (us). Stress places the adolescent brain in a constant state of agitation. (See Stress and the Adolescent Brain, page 51.)

So we burnish one more skill set: that of Mitigator. By our children's adolescence, we are still needed to soften the pain of a bruised shin or ego or feeling. But we are also uniquely positioned as both the cause of, and the relief from, the stresses that threaten to hold their formative brains hostage. By recognizing the causes, we help develop the cures that hopefully lead to prevention.

Even highly reactive babies—born, it seems, anxiety prone—can learn to live with and relieve the stresses that dog them. Once learned, these soothing tricks of the coping trade calm the most hair-triggered stressors, like epinephrine to a bee sting. Let's look at a few potential relievers.

STRESS MITIGATORS

FREQUENT STRESSORS	SUCCESSFUL MITIGATORS
School work, especially deadlines: tests, quizzes, papers, presentations	Step 1: Help them get to know their demons *and* the accompanying stress reactions (e.g., so afraid of failing, they procrastinate; as the deadline approaches, they become paralyzed by the mounting workload; when they try to attack it, they can't remember a thing.)

STRESS MITIGATORS

FREQUENT STRESSORS	SUCCESSFUL MITIGATORS
	Step 2: Expose the stress demons to daylight. *So what happens when you feel like there's too much to study? What does it feel like?* Step 3: Problem solve with mitigators: *How about you . . .* • Write down study/draft-writing schedule • Build in extra time for relaxation, play • Find the words to "talk yourself out of the fear," like a mantra Step 4: Rehearse and remind (gently) rather than demand. **Help them learn how they learn.**
Generally overwhelmed	**Step 1: Talk about the difference between "chilling" and "killing time":** • *Chilling* (i.e., time for quiet, internal exploration) fosters creativity, reflection, sharpens focus (think yoga or meditation) • *Killing time* is procrastination (see step 1 under School Work Mitigators)

	Step 2: Reinforce daydreaming about self and future (outside of class, that is); exercises the imagination, improves relationships, fosters abstract thinking **Step 3: Slow down! (That includes us.) The more we run in all directions, the more they'll think they should, too. Nothing breeds calm like calm; nothing breeds stress like stress.** **It's harder to tack into the wind than with it.**
Sad, lonely, homesick	Step 1: Don't demand perfection. Instead, reward hard work. The former leads to the development of a false self, built to please. The latter leads to an authentic self, built to cope. Step 2: Reinforce rituals (e.g., family dinners, favorite meals, games). The familiar is like an embrace to the adolescent psyche. Step 3: Be available to hang— their way. **Emotional closeness and warmth, espcially with adults, builds powerful connections that actually help alleviate stress.**

STRESS MITIGATORS	
FREQUENT STRESSORS	**SUCCESSFUL MITIGATORS**
	Step 4: Reinforce friendships— they actually repair stress damage. Step 5: Do the "3 Good Things" exercise with them every day for a week (and then as needed): • _____ made me feel good today. • I appreciate _____. • Something I learned or that went well is _____. **Gratefulness: A common element among the happy.**
All Stressors	**SLEEP!** Sleep fortifies the brain against stress; lack of it impairs everything from judgment to concentration to impulse control (see Sleep and the Adolescent Brain, page 50). The term *sleep on it* has special meaning for adolescents.

In increasing amounts, and in alarming ways, stress harms the adolescent brain. If anxiety and depression are diseases, then stress is their viral counterpart. From school work, to sports, to tryouts, to home life, few aspects of an adolescent's life are stress free. Inside our parenting first aid kits, we carry mitigators as antidotes.

4. Make Patience Your Best Ally

From a perch, either figuratively or often literally taller than we are, our adolescents spread feckless wings and take off, often straight into unanticipated temptations and/or emotions. Eventually we learn to accept the resulting turbulence, the ignored directionals, our overtaxed patience. No wonder that even the best of us snap, at some point, over some (often silly) thing. Snaps, though not always preventable, rarely solve whatever problem causes them. Regardless of how plentiful or meager our supplies of patience, there is always room for more when it comes to dealing with an adolescent. One way to replenish, or at least conserve, a dwindling supply is the *double-or-nothing* tactic. Here's how it works:

> **US:** *Hi, honey. What's up?*
> **THEM:** *Well, I know I said I'd be home in about twenty minutes, but I'm going to be a few minutes late.*
> **US:** *So what time will you be home?*
> **THEM:** *Probably in about half an hour . . .*
> **US:** *Okay, thanks for calling [*or whatever response is warranted, as that's not the point being made here*].*
> *We'll be waiting.*

Do wait. Do watch. Do double the amount of time allotted. The *double-or-nothing* tactic is not about correcting irregular or undesirable behavior patterns. In fact, its use presupposes a generally consistent adherence to the Rules of Play. Think of *double-or-nothing* as a parental prophylactic, a patience preserver for when we suspect that our adolescents are in the clutches of a brain tussle, or are possibly trying to yank our already overextended chains.

Here's another example of *double-or-nothing* at work:

> **US:** *I know Red's parents are away and I know his parents don't allow him to have parties when they're away.*
> **THEM:** *It's not a party; it's just a few kids: me, Brittany, Greg, and Lacy. That's all.*
> **US:** *But how do you know that's all?*
> **THEM:** *Cuz I know! He doesn't want anyone else to come over!*

Whatever the reported number: double it (at least). Then decide whether to sanction the plan.

And another example:

> **THEM:** *But I only have a little more homework: one more subject. I'll be off the phone in a minute. I promise. This is really important; she's really upset.*
> **US:** *Okay, I'll check back in five more minutes.*

Do wait. Do count. Do double how much homework is left (or if they say none) and the time until the end of the phone call.

Why allow such (apparent) indulgences? Because we understand so much more than they think we do. Because it's not about us—and it's not (or shouldn't be) about precision (unless it's explicitly about that). There is nothing precise about the havoc being wreaked in the adolescent brain (remember the construction site image?). It's about understanding what makes *them* tick so we can all synchronize our watches. It's about giving the prefrontal cortex enough leeway to learn to quell the uprising, rather than us doing so.

Our storehouses contain (or should) a much greater supply of patience than theirs do. How else will they learn when to call up reserves, other than by watching us? Are we advocating not holding them to agreements? Absolutely not. We're just introducing little surge protectors like *double-or-nothing*, designed to help us stay in control—of us. After all, why should they abide by the Rules of Play if we can't?

5. Model the Three-Pronged Approach: Consistency, Predictability, and Stability

Like deepening wrinkles, parenting an adolescent requires us to face many ineluctable realities. Two more to add to the list include:

- As they charge full speed ahead, the parental face will be the first, and most lasting, image our adolescents see in their rearview mirrors. Not the media. Not their peers. Not their first loves.
- As eager as we are to be liberated from this adolescence-induced parental limbo, they are even more eager to be liberated from us.

These two realities, in many ways, form the paradox of parenting an adolescent: They can't live with us and they can't live without us. So where does that leave us—other than caught in the middle? It leaves us as the ones who understand best the internal struggles of our adolescents; the ones willing to sort the limbic-driven logic from the prefrontal-cortex-driven logic; the only ones able to take multiple hits from errant reasoning and still love them unconditionally. There's often only one other thing standing in our way: us.

> **US:** *I'm sure you've heard the stories circulating about the group of eighth graders having oral sex in the back of the bus on their way home from a school trip?*
> **THEM:** *Yeah, so? It happens all the time.*

US: *What do you mean it happens all the time? I'd better not ever catch you doing something like that! Not only is it disgusting, it's unhealthy and degrading. If I ever find out that you've been involved in something like this . . .*

While this position may express strong, honest, and even reliable feelings, watch how quickly its sharp edge severs any sort of communication. Assuming that connection is a desired objective, even a minor explosion can crater a good intention.

When in doubt about what to say, or think, ask that one simple question: *What do I* really *care about?* For example, if the answer in this case is safety from STDs and/or (self) respect, then make that the chorus, even while filling in the verses.

Let's try this one again:

US: *I'm sure you've heard the stories circulating about the group of eighth graders having oral sex in the back of the bus on their way home from a school trip?*
THEM: *Yeah, so? It happens all the time.*
US: *You know what's scariest to me about this? That these kids don't seem to realize how unsafe oral sex really is; those who weren't using some kind of protection could easily get an STD.*
THEM: *I know; we learned about that in health classes at school.*
US: *You know, I don't know how to think about this oral sex thing. To me, it's one of the most intimate things you can do with a person. I read something like this and it feels like to these kids it's a game.*
THEM: *It's not the same as with you. Kids just do it. It's no big deal.*

US: *That's what it sounds like. Do you think that's because kids aren't scared of getting an STD, so they think it's okay to have oral sex anywhere, anytime?*

When adolescents feel safe from ambush or censorship, they'll usually respond. And most actually like to show off their newly minted reasoning powers—even, no especially, to us. When they feel heard, their responses are generally honest. Honesty begets honesty. Anger begets anger. Consistency begets predictability, which can beget stability. This is how the brain makes its connections. This is how we can help. At least this is how we keep the conversation going.

When our adolescents sneak looks at us for direction, which they do—all the time—what do we want them to see? How about how hard we've worked to get it right, even if it's taken more than one try; how soundly we've reasoned, despite pressure to the contrary; and how responsibly we've behaved, even when, not if, we've made a wrong turn? Not afraid to show some sweat, some pain, even some remorse, we model consistency, predictability, and stability throughout endless round-the-clock shifts.

TRUTH IS AS MALLEABLE AS THEIR FRIDAY NIGHT PLANS

FROM AN EARLY AGE, CHILDREN SENSE THE POWER OF WORDS as surely as they sense the threat of danger. Simple monosyllabic commands magically lead to results. As our children track the responses and reactions to each new action, they realize that a simple word (like *no*) can change an entire experience, a changed experience can alter an entire reaction, an altered reaction can form a whole new impression.

But not until adolescence do they come to understand more fully the significant role that truth plays in their lives. With help from new brain resources, compliments of a developing prefrontal cortex, they begin to comprehend more fully that truth is neither binary nor unassailable. In fact, the connective tissue between intention and expression is often far more gray than black and white (see chapter 1, Their Brains Are to Blame). While learning to respect truth as the royalty of virtues, they also learn how to justify its betrayal.

To understand this dichotomy is to understand why adolescents lie.

The Anatomy of an Adolescent Lie

TRUTH TO ADOLESCENTS IS OFTEN AS MALLEABLE AS THEIR Friday night plans. If a position, desire, or demand is defensible, it must be true. And as anyone who has ever wrangled with an adolescent knows, almost anything is defensible.

> **US:** *You said you were going to John's house to watch a movie, but you end up at a party at a total stranger's house and his parents were out of town?*
> **THEM:** *I didn't know that we were going to go to the party when I went to John's. It just came up. That's not lying! Anyway, you've said yourself that you used to go lots of places that your parents didn't know about.*

Note of caution: Lest we think that exposing some of our own hard-earned adolescent battle scars will raise our cool quotient in their eyes, it won't. Since many of us participated in or observed some fairly radical behavioral experiments in our own teens and early twenties, it may be tempting to offer up some seemingly harmless recollections of our own less-than-responsible behaviors. Figure that any shared transgression runs a fifty-fifty chance of finding its way into the enabling rather than inhibiting column of possible adolescent behaviors. And once we reveal past follies, our adolescents' expert lie-detection capabilities will reject any transparent attempts at retraction or renunciation. So before rushing to report any of our tainted histories, we might first analyze the result we're after.

> **US:** *You're right; I did that when I was your age. And in retrospect, I probably shouldn't have because it isn't something to be proud of. I definitely made some mistakes*

and bad decisions when I was young, things I now realize were stupid. [Translation: I, too, am human.] But here's what scares me about your situation . . .

Detour taken and acknowledged, then back to the point. If they press for more, don't lie or deny, simply continue to acknowledge that everyone makes mistakes, and each one harbors a lesson.

In many ways, how we preach and practice truth defines our moral character and nourishes our self-respect. Not so with our adolescents. For them, truth has taken a different form: a means to an end. Adolescents justify their versions of the truth with impunity, mimicking a host of public and private role models from almost every walk of life. More so than any preceding generation, our adolescents have witnessed truth being sacrificed at the altar of self-service, entertainment, or, worse, personal and political ambition. For our adolescents, to be caught lying is not a sign of failed integrity; rather, it's a sign of their failure to lie *well*. Indeed a recent survey of more than thirty thousand high school students reveals that 83 percent admit lying to parents about something significant. And yet 96 percent say it is important that people trust them.[1]

But we all told lies when we were their age, we confess. *So what's so different about our kids?*

Since they were old enough to sit still in front of a TV, DVD, or computer, we docked them in a harbor we assumed to be safe, grateful for the free child-care services provided by the media or electronic marketplace. Happy to have one less ball to juggle, if only for a time slot, we entrusted them to the subliminal layering of unfiltered messages and unvetted companions. As a result, they have imbibed models and norms more reflective of a screenwriter's (questionable) values than our own. Too busy or too trusting to taste-test a host of unsa-

vory plotlines, we unwittingly aided and abetted their growing dependency on a steady diet of situational disrespect and
compromised truths, often reinforced by an artificial laugh
track and endorsed by a surrogate family of peers.

> **US:** *You realize that those kids were taking advantage of*
> *each other in that episode, right?*
> **THEM:** *Yeah, yeah, I know. Don't worry, I would never*
> *act that way.*

Perhaps unintentionally, many of us may have introduced
our adolescents to variations on the truth theme. Few of us
can deny practicing the art of linguistic nuance to navigate
around hurt feelings and avoid petty nuisances. Nor can we
protect our adolescents from a steady stream of public displays
of dishonesty, from trumped-up rationalizations for adultery
or military aggression to some of the practices of our coun-
try's once exalted business leaders. And that's before they turn
on the television. All the more reason that our private conversations with our adolescents should focus not on *whether* they
are telling the truth but on *why* they should be.

Is it any wonder that, in their search for reliable models of
integrity, our adolescents might gravitate toward voices that
more closely echo their own? After all, who better to understand and support them than their peers? What better way to
win the approval of peers than to conform? From this arc of
influence, and under the new management of a rapidly
changing brain, they often view adults as forces to be reck-
oned with, or circumvented, more than trusted advisers. Suddenly, the moral high ground we once held firmly has
buckled under the weight of our own fallibility. We are suddenly accused of not knowing or understanding them, of
being out of touch—and maybe we are. So our penance be-

comes learning to accept our adolescents for who they have become, not the children they once were.

CATEGORIES OF LIES

LEFT STANDING ON THE RECEIVING END OF SO MANY DEAD-ended conversations with our adolescents, we notice that comments or reactions that used to strike on target seem to sail right by them, unnoticed or ignored. Meanwhile, our adolescents nonchalantly cast aside our queries, warnings, even threats, like an outgrown shoe. And we wonder why they look at us as if we are total strangers commanding them to provide answers they often aren't even aware of possessing. Perhaps we should not be surprised that (now that they know they can) they pick and choose what *they* want *us* to know, as chiefs of their own bureaus of intelligence. Maybe by with-holding information (that is, the truth), they are merely protecting what they believe to be rightfully theirs.

> **US:** *What happened to that new jacket I bought you?*
> **THEM:** *It's at school.*
> **US:** *Do you know where at school?*
> **THEM:** *Don't worry about it; it's mine. If it's lost, it's my problem, not yours.*

The ways in which our adolescents manipulate what they want us to know fall into three general categories: *omissions, distortions,* and, of course, *outright fabrications.* Although each one crosses over the honesty line, clearly outright fabrication strays the farthest. Frequently defended as not "real lying," fib mongering is usually driven by some kind of task or responsibility avoidance or privacy protection designed to spare

them from such discomforts as consequences, shame, or embarrassment. Regardless of the particular strain of mistruth, if
left undetected or unaddressed, it can spread easily.

Let's explore the three categories more closely.

1. Omissions

> **US:** *I thought we had an understanding about going on
> Facebook before your homework was finished.*
> **THEM:** *I was just getting a homework assignment. I'm
> getting off right now.*

What may well have begun as a noble cause (such as getting a homework assignment) can be easily corrupted for a
host of well-intentioned reasons. Bearing in mind the slipper-
iness of the accusation slope, we simply proclaim omissions
for what they are, lest we be taken for a dupe. We do so with
conviction and move on. Anything more breeds contempt.

> **US:** *I want you to have what you need to do your work;
> that's your job. But taking advantage of the situation is not
> showing respect for what we agreed on, nor is it
> demonstrating the kind of responsibility that earns you more
> freedom and flexibility. My intention is not to shut you off
> from Facebook, but I need to know that you are upholding
> your end of the bargain by not cheating or sneaking.*

2. Distortions (or Half-Truths)

Let's replay an earlier conversation:

> **US:** *You said you were going to John's house to watch a
> movie, but you end up at a party at a total stranger's house
> and his parents were out of town?*

THEM: *I didn't* know *that we were going to go to the party when I went to John's. It just came up. That's not lying! Anyway, you've said yourself that you used to go lots of places that your parents didn't know about.*

US: *As you know, I wasn't there, so I don't know what was supposed to happen or what really did happen. All I know and can rely on is what we agreed upon. Not only is staying at a party with no adults present potentially dangerous, but it isn't being respectful of that person's home or parents, either.*

(Notice the use of the word *staying*. In the multiscreen age we live in, small gatherings can quickly mushroom into unruly parties.) A key to staying safe is attuning our teenagers to certain signals and circumstances that should trigger safety alarms.

The earlier a warning system gets installed into the adolescent psyche, the better the chances they will learn to rely on it. Recognizing perils or threats to their safety may be as important as avoiding them.

THEM: *It wasn't even a party. It was just a few kids hanging out. Even if some kids brought beer, no one was out of control, not even close.*

US: *What if someone drank more than they realized and passed out? What would you have done?*

THEM: *No one who was there was like that. That just wasn't going to happen!*

US: *Maybe not this time. But what if it did? What would you do?*

Like omissions, distortions weigh in on a different scale from outright fabrications (remember the *double-or-nothing* tactic in chapter 1, Their Brains Are to Blame). The only way to really know the difference between a distortion and an outright fabrication is to keep the conversation going long enough to form an opinion—not necessarily about the nature of the manipulated truth, but whether the Rules of Play have been upheld. That's the common ground.

3. Outright Fabrications

We often cling to the fantasy that truth telling is a genetic trait and guilt and remorse are its natural defenders. They aren't. Moral relativism has the insidious capacity to subtly squeeze the integrity right out of any situation. Everybody lies, so why shouldn't we? If we do, why shouldn't our adolescents think they can? Who among us can claim never to have fibbed to a solicitor, or sported an article of knocked-off designer clothing, or fabricated an excuse to get out of something? There is no denying that our adolescents have been weaned on half-truths. No wonder they don't notice any bitter aftertaste.

GETTING AT THE TRUTH

SO HOW DO WE GET THE TRUTH FROM OUR ADOLESCENTS? First, we don't ask for it unless we are ready to hear it. If we can't control our reaction to reports of drinking, drugs, sex, skipping school, plagiarizing, and other such transgressions, then we won't ever hear about them, at least not voluntarily. Is silence really a true indicator of smooth sailing? How do we know?

Second, we ask how much we need to know versus want to know. Are we primarily concerned that they know how to stay safe? Or do we want to know whether they are actually partaking? Is it our right to know, or our obligation? Are we just curious? Is knowing tantamount to controlling? Or is knowing the first step to helping? The truth we seek remains buried until, and unless, it can survive the scrutiny of our spotlight. But scrutiny usually implies intensity. What to us feels like concern, to them feels like heat. The more heat we apply, the more they pull away, drawn to their much cooler friends.

> **US:** *How can I trust you if I don't know whether you're telling the truth?*
> **THEM:** *How can I tell the truth, if you won't trust that I'll do the right thing? Just because there's alcohol at a party doesn't mean I'll get drunk.*

Truth, trust, fairness, and honesty are noble concepts and do represent what's at stake—but we are not Platos and they are not Aristotles. Polemics may be fun and good mental exercise, at least for the stimulation-craving teenage brain. But trust is something an adolescent needs to earn, and understanding truth as an absolute requires a more fully formed sense of morality that comes from experience and—yes—experimenting, as well as a more developed prefrontal cortex.

> **US:** *I believe you, and as long as you don't give me any reason to doubt it, I trust your integrity. But it's my job to watch—closely—and determine as best I can whether the Rules of Play are being upheld. Your job is to convince me that you are doing your part. If you give me reason to doubt you, or the plan, then my alarm bells will go off and security will automatically tighten. It's up to you.*

Assuming we are honest ourselves (and they know if we're not), then our adolescents know that honesty is something we value. Beyond that, we often know more about what we don't know about our adolescents than what we do know. We know that they can argue ardently on behalf of a point of view (even if they don't really believe it) or a neglected chore, but are often tight-lipped when it comes to talking about their day or their friends or their worries. We know much more about what they think is wrong with us, and their lives, than we do about what they believe is right. Much of what we know, we gather from crumbs of conversations inadvertently strewn in our paths—which is why we have to keep on the lookout.

The only way to avoid becoming mired in the devilish details of teenage shenanigans is to constantly ask ourselves what we really care most about as adults responsible for their well-being. The answer should be that we want them to come home safely, to be part of our lives, and to be appreciated as good people.

Like it or not, experience and experimenting are the growth hormones of adolescents. And while we nourish this growth, we must also manage it. We do that by relying on the three Rules of Play, which we hang on to as if they were our last thread of connection to our adolescents, our three moments of truth.

To get the truth, we invoke a quid pro quo: You work with me and I'll work with you.

HOW TO DEAL

1. Listen first, react second.

2. Don't accuse; redirect.

3. Be honest ourselves.

4. Expect the truth, but be prepared not to get it.

5. Keep the issues concrete.

1. Listen First, React Second

Don your most stoic expression and steel yourself to the possibility of hearing about irresponsible driving, sex (oral and more), marijuana (and more), unsupervised parties, bad grades, sneaking, stealing, cheating—and more. Does this mean your adolescents have or will partake in all this? If they haven't, then they certainly are exposed to it. Does this mean that kids we know and care about—or worse, kids of friends of ours—might be involved? Quite likely. Once unleashed, truth does not discern. Without regard for feelings or diplomacy, truth can expose many an adolescent reality, toppling defenses and shattering closely held beliefs. Our job is to listen closely so we can hear it.

> **US:** *Hi sweetie, how was the party?*
> **THEM:** *Fine. It was fun. I'm tired; I'm going to bed.*
> **US:** *Okay. See you in the morning.*

Though we may note some erratic or inconsistent behavior, we wait; it's late and tomorrow is another, clearer day.

Remember, the moment we become an adversary, the truth becomes whitewashed.

Sometime later:

US: *So who was at the party?*
THEM: *A bunch of kids. Look, you might get a call from some parents.*
US: *Really? Why?*
THEM: *Well, actually some kids were drinking at the party and Steve's parents came home and were pretty mad.*

Sometimes the pressure of a hidden truth becomes too much, causing a slow leak or even an outburst. In either case, we try not to stop the flow but wait it out, trying to assess the extent of the damage. At appropriate pauses, we carefully insert clarifying questions aimed at answering the two questions that matter most: What really happened? And what is this confession telling us about general patterns of behavior?

US: *Was this the first time something like this has happened to you?*

Since truth missions like this one have no predictable beginning or ending, once launched, they should remain opportunistic and head straight to the point.

THEM: *No . . . not really . . .*
US: *For alcohol, or drugs too?*
THEM: *A few other times I guess . . .*

Would this information have come out without the fear of bigger trouble than our consequences? Maybe not. Are we getting the level of detail we really want? Probably not. Are we getting enough to know how to proceed? That's where we aim.

Think of each truth our adolescents reveal to us as one more in a long string of parenting tests. In each case, we face three choices: We can pretend whatever it was didn't happen; we can smother the disclosure with blankets of indignation; or we can nurture the truth in the hope of spawning more.

> **US:** *I'm really glad you're telling me about all this, so we can work out how to respond. What should I expect to hear if I do get a call?*
>
> **THEM:** *I'm not sure.* [Note the omission.]
>
> **US:** *What do you think I should do?*
>
> **THEM:** *Let's just wait to see what happens, okay? Maybe nothing will.*
>
> **US:** *We can do that, but in the meantime, I know you know that you have broken a trust, not to mention a Rule of Play.*
>
> **THEM:** *I knew I shouldn't have told you. I knew you'd get mad!*
>
> **US:** *I'm actually not mad.* [And the reason that this is an unassailable truth is that our manner remains remarkably calm, though somber.] *But I am disappointed. Not that you told me the truth. Because I would have been very angry had I learned about this from someone else. I'm disappointed that you weren't able to stick to the Rules of Play. But at least now we can work this out together, which in the end will be much less painful—for both of us. Have there been other times when you've jeopardized safety?*

Note the timing of this question: For every truth card we play, we expect them to play one in return. Like seasoned cardsharps, we keep our emotions in check, determined not to fold first.

> **THEM:** *I don't know. How should I know? . . . Maybe.*
> **US:** *Well, what's most important to me is that I understand enough about what's going on so that we can talk it through. But right now, I'm not sure I know enough to even do that.*
> **THEM:** *Well, it's not like I'm drunk every weekend, or anything. You're freaking out over nothing!*
> **US:** *Look, I know that this kind of thing goes on, and a lot of kids are involved. And now I know that you are, too, which is better than you having to lie about it. Putting yourself in a situation where you get caught like this is not staying safe whether you were actually drinking or not. And if someone had had an accident after leaving that party, Steve's entire family could have been held liable. That's not showing respect for Steve, or his parents.*

We welcome any opportunity that allows our adolescents to walk away from the wreckage of a bad decision safely. Even better is any opportunity that pits the merits of telling the truth against the adolescent tendency toward self-preservation.

> **US:** *I would probably never have known about this without the threat of Steve's parents calling, right?*
> **THEM:** *Right.*
> **US:** *Then I'm even more glad this happened. Now at least I know what we're dealing with. Let's see what happens. And then we'll decide on the appropriate consequences. Somehow, though, I'm sensing that there's more that needs to come out. Though this is not over, it's at least a start.*

TRANSLATION: *I know there is more that you haven't told me [omissions]. I'm willing to wait it out.*

Sometimes, if we sense that the truth is slow to emerge, the best way to purge it may be to wait for a designated, but not extended, period of time—say, a day or so. Most adolescents are well acquainted with the methods of confession that lead most expeditiously to forgiveness, even if accompanied by a consequence. Much more ominous to them is the thought of our lingering disapproval or intensified scrutiny. So we invoke one of most effective antidotes to adolescent prevarications: patience. Patience, coupled with disappointment and a profound understanding of the power of silence, affords us the opportunity to listen first and react second. In doing so, we communicate that the truth is worth waiting for, but only for so long. If, after a time (our discretion), the truth doesn't come out, we cite the Rules of Play and invoke the consequence(s) that we've had ample time to contemplate.

2. Don't Accuse; Redirect

Remember that at this point in their lives, truth has meaning only in the context of the moment. It is a means to an end.

US: *I thought you were going to Adam's house to study; you didn't mention that a bunch of kids were going to be there.*
THEM: *What difference does it make? And anyway, we did study.*

If our goal is to stay connected, why disconnect by getting hung up on an accusation or our own rigidity? Why not use the connection to build more? It is much harder to lie to people we trust than those we don't. This may explain why our adolescents try so hard to distance themselves from us. If they don't, it is too difficult to separate enough to test our limits. And unless they test our limits, they may never come to know their own.

> **US:** *How can I let you go next time when I can't count on you to tell me what's really going on? This is a school night; you told me you were going to study. It sounds to me as though it turned into something else. Am I right?*
> **THEM:** *What's the problem? We all needed to study, and we did. I wasn't sure who was going to be there. It's not my house; it's not up to me who gets invited over.*
> **US:** *I just had a different understanding about the situation. While I believe that you had some studying to do, it sounds to me like that wasn't your priority. For me to trust you, I need to know that you are being straight and respecting our rules [*for instance, school nights are for doing homework]. *This is playing by the Rules of Play.*
> **TRANSLATION:** *If you want special privileges, you need to earn them. You do that by* not *making me question you or my trust in you.*

Meanwhile, we report any betrayals of trust as fact, unencumbered by emotion or preaching. We keep our expectations clear and stay focused on them, *not* the details. While righteous indignation may be our right, it rarely rights a wrong. Unless we want them to doubt our truth.

3. Be Honest Ourselves

If they see *us* drinking and driving, think about the message (especially since a recent study found that adolescents who have seen their parents drunk are two times more likely to get drunk in a typical month.[2]) If they see us use even the most benign excuse to get out of something, even a telemarketer, think about the message. If we tip *our* truth scales, why shouldn't they tip theirs?

> **THEM:** *Why did you lie about our ages?*
> **US:** *It wasn't really a lie. It saved us a lot of money. This trip is expensive enough. We need the money more than the airlines do.*

Most of the time, our own shoddily constructed truths, especially in support of the family good, survive their own usefulness. When young, our children have no need to question or compare our versions of the truth against anyone else's. But all that changes once they discover the existence of other points of view (that is, adolescence). Suddenly, every truth and dissemblance reflects a different situational topography with its own contours and dimensions. Perhaps the best way to get the truth from our adolescents is to make it hard for them to lie to us. We do that by constantly working to show respect and keep in touch. The best way to do that is to be honest ourselves.

There is, however, an important caution regarding truth telling to a pre-adult child. Some business is and should remain adult business, such as divorce and child custody. However tempted we may be to involve our children in these matters, they are often too weighty for them to bear. Revealing too much runs the risk of rendering permanent damage to the all-important adolescent identity-formation process. To prevent interference with this process requires a careful balancing of the truth scales.

> **THEM:** *Why are you so angry with Dad? What did he do to make you hate him?*
> **US:** *He did something awful, and hurt me very badly.*

Although this may well be the honest truth, it is like handing them a piece of dry ice that they can neither hold on to nor let go of.

Now consider a different approach:

> **THEM:** *Why are you so angry with Dad? What did he do to make you hate him?*
> **US:** *You are right, I am angry at the moment, but I don't hate him, and anyway this is not something you need to worry about; it's between Daddy and me. I'll be okay in a moment; and we're working it out.*

4. Expect the Truth, but Be Prepared Not to Get It

At first doubt, decide whether our adolescents have transgressed one of the agreed-upon Rules of Play (stay safe, show respect, keep in touch), or whether they have merely touched a nerve (say, a friend you fear is a bad influence, a bad grade, a messy room) before addressing the deed.

Next, if they have transgressed a Rule of Play, do impose a consequence, but keep it as specific, finite (a beginning and an end), enforceable, and related to the transgression as possible (both in magnitude and in form). A consequence rarely prevents a bad deed from reoccurring; it merely reinforces a dawning adolescent discovery: actions, both good and bad, come with consequences. The key is not to overuse any one (like cell phone deprivation). Getting them to link (behavioral) cause to effect beats getting them to blame us as the (root) cause any day.

Listed below are some common adolescent infractions as well as some ideas for an accompanying consequence. Note: If and when adolescents are driving, by the way, then car privileges can supersede almost any other consequence, with the possible exception of their cell phone appendages. However, abuse of cell phones or texting while driving ranks right up there with drinking, invoking both the physical and staying out of trouble categories of the Stay Safe Rules of Play.

INFRACTION: Lying/sneaking.
CONSEQUENCE: Apology and special favors to the transgressed. This is especially effective if the recipients are outside the family.

INFRACTION: Missed curfew.
CONSEQUENCE: Lost opportunity to participate in the next desired event(s), or docked time on the next outing.

INFRACTION: Disrespect/rudeness/attitude.
CONSEQUENCE: This is a tough one because: (a) sometimes their brains are literally to blame for their overreactions, and we want the storm to pass as quickly as it blew in; (b) the more we fight them, the more we tend to sink into the quicksand of their convoluted logic; and (c) many consequences impose more of a burden on us to enforce than on them to endure.

Consequences in this case should come only after trying every conceivable method to dissipate said attitude—such as, humor, distraction, reason, and so on. If the attitude persists, then try:

- Isolation, time alone to think about it—the adolescent version of a time-out. Not recommended for the already isolated adolescent.
- A positive (extra) contribution to family life or the victim of the rage (perhaps a desired or needed favor such as that person's chores).
- Lost opportunity to participate in the next desired event(s).

INFRACTION: Irresponsibility, a forgotten or misplaced commitment of some kind.
CONSEQUENCE: Double duty around the situation. For an unmade bed, then, bed entirely stripped, with bedding left in a heap; unemptied trash might lead to scrubbing out the trash cans; disregard for belongings (such as steady stream of lost or misplaced articles) could mean a docked allowance or repayment in the form of manual labor.

INFRACTION: Too much texting, TV, Internet, or what have you.
CONSEQUENCE: Lost privileges in those areas. Note that although it may be obvious, abuse of cell phones, computers, game devices, and so forth, located in their rooms or places where they offer unfair temptation are our problem, not theirs. We might as well offer a drink to a recovering alcoholic.

INFRACTION: Taking advantage of parental absence.

CONSEQUENCE: This is grave enough to go right to grounding, but consider adding extra home-related duties that send the message that disrespect toward us and our home will lead to more contributions in this particular area.

INFRACTION: Not keeping in touch.

CONSEQUENCE: If they already have a cell phone, this is easy: Confiscate it for a prescribed period of time. But a confiscated cell phone, or no cell phone, does not condone losing touch. Today's adolescent is never far from some form of keyboard communication, their own or a friend's, so an inability to check in, a bit more frequently if need be, is as likely as the dog actually chowing down on their homework. If confiscation fails, respectfully require them to stay in (again, for a prescribed period of time). Note: Beware of allowing them to buy something with their own money and then assert that possession is nine-tenths of the law. *Before* sanctioning any purchase that could affect adherence to the Rules of Play (car, Smartphone, computer, iPod, and the like), establish usage ground rules. One such ground rule might be that any purchase they make, even with their own funds, while in our care, falls under the jurisdiction of the Rules of Play. Therefore, from our point of view, the primary use of a cell phone, regardless of how it was funded, is to keep in touch. If that responsibility gets overlooked, then the cell phone becomes our possession, for a prescribed period of time.

Again, the purpose of a consequence should be to reinforce the Rules of Play. Like a homing pigeon, consequences should both launch from and come back to the Rules of Play. Direct, straightforward, and minimal, the Rules of Play obviate the need for unenforceable rules that are easy to break and easier to lie about. Do the Rules of Play guarantee truth? No, but they do provide a focal point, a demilitarized zone from which to negotiate and connect.

Despite what our adolescents might think, or accuse us of, inflicting and enforcing consequences is as appealing to us as a trip to the dentist. Why not share the discomfort and involve them in the consequences discussion? After all, they have to live with them. We need only approve.

Here are some additional tips that may help dole and enforce consequences:

- Leave a clear escalation path so there is somewhere to go if the initial try (or tries) fails.
- Don't waste time on rules that are unenforceable; it gives parenting a bad name.
- Beware of groundings, especially consecutive sentences. They can be more of a punishment for us than for them. The more sparingly we use them, the more impact they will wield. But once delivered, we need to stick to them!
- Beware, in particular, of grounding for special events, such as proms, big games (in which they are supposed to play), and so forth. They can and will be used against us—sometimes for life!
- Refrain from nagging, piling on, or gloating. If they know that consequences follow unacceptable behavior (provided fair warning has been given), then a simple warning will suffice, followed by a calmly rendered verdict. Any retaliatory behavior simply results in a more serious consequence.

■ Don't be afraid to be creative! The more outlandish yet appropriate the consequences, the better the chances that our adolescents will remember them—and try to avoid the same fate in the future. Creative consequences can pack a punch while sparing us the task of having to continually enforce painful punishments. (Despite the wailing, our teenagers might even glimpse the humor.)

THEM: *You said it was okay to have a friend over while you were gone. Then Carly called and she just wanted to drop something off. I didn't know the others were with her. I was going to tell you after I cleaned things up.*
US: *We agreed you could have one friend over. But it's not showing respect to me or our rules that you ended up with a bunch of kids who clearly don't have the same respect for our home as we do, and then you chose not to tell me about it. I'll tell you what. We're having the Harkers and the Roeses over tonight; why don't you stay in and help me serve and clean up. By the way, that's a nonnegotiable.*
TRANSLATION: *It's simple. We agreed. You broke the agreement. I don't like doling out the consequences any more than you like receiving them. But when you don't respect others, our home, or me, there has to be a consequence.*

5. Keep the Issues Concrete

US: *This is not about whether or not I trust you; it's about me feeling okay that you are making good decisions. Your sister said you didn't pick her up at school as we agreed.*

Note the use of *we agreed* instead of *I asked*. When taking aim, always target mutual responsibility.

> **THEM:** *It was fine! I got her a way home. She didn't mind at all. [*Note the use of distortion.*]*
>
> **US:** *I actually don't know how she felt about it because she's protecting you. But what I'm concerned about right now is that the plans we agreed upon changed and you didn't stay in touch about it.*
>
> **TRANSLATION:** *If I know what you're up to, I can ask the questions I need to feel okay. Without the opportunity to satisfy my concerns, I'm going to worry that you are either trying to hide something [use omissions], or making an unsafe decision.*

In other words, we try to convey that while they can fool us some of the time, they can't all of the time.

> **THEM:** *Look, I promised that I'd stay and help Jake out. I made sure she had a way home. [*Another use of omission.*] It all worked out. What's the big deal?*
>
> **US:** *I appreciate that you took my request seriously, but here's what I'm concerned about: I entrusted this task to you, not someone else. When you displace my trust onto someone else, I no longer feel assured of her safety, or respect for our agreement—and most important, she doesn't necessarily feel entirely safe. None of these situations is fair to me or to her. I need to know that I can trust you to do what you say you're going to do.*
>
> **TRANSLATION:** *Reward the sense of responsibility but be clear about the issue. And convince me that you can make good choices.*

THEM: *Look, I said I'd get her home and I did.* [Omission.]

US: *I understand that you wanted to help Jake and I hope you understand why I'm upset about you not living up to your end of the deal. I need a little time to think about this and the consequences. We'll talk more later.*

THEM: *No, I don't understand!* [Distortion, at the least.] *Why are you so upset? She got home, okay? Why does there have to be a consequence?*

US: *Here's what concerns me: What if something had happened to her on the way home? I wouldn't have known where she was or who she was with. I also wouldn't have known where you were and why you two weren't together.*

Consequences are what happen when you make bad decisions. That's enough for now; we'll talk more later. I need time to think about it.

TRANSLATION: *And so do you.*

We steady ourselves for a (final, we hope) round of verbal indignations as their arsenal of defenses (in this case) nears empty. Secure in our stance, we hold on to the only response that, in this case, will never betray us: We say *nothing*.

CONTROLLING THEM IS NOT THE POINT

THE ESSENCE OF PARENTING AN ADOLESCENT IS THE SHIFTING locus of control. The sooner we relinquish control over our adolescents as a parental right, the faster *they* will take command of their lives.

One of our most natural parenting instincts is to tighten our hold on that which we feel slipping out of our control, whether the cause is a toddler's tantrums or the activities of an adolescent. In fact, many of us target control over our adolescents as one of our defining parental missions. We rely on control as the best method to realize our own expectations, as well as the antidote for a host of adolescent problems and violations, from insolence to indolence.

Regardless of our motives, the potency and effectiveness of our control mechanisms seem to decline as our children age, perhaps from oversaturation or merely an age-appropriate buildup of resistance. Unable to stop the seepage, we often frantically search for more variations on the same control theme. Sometimes these themes equate to heightened security measures, or tightened friendship bonds. Regardless of how reasonable, clever, intractable, or threatening our methods of control, a determined adolescent can wriggle from their clutches. Rather than viewing control as something we do *to* them, we look for ways to work *with* them. Like water, we let control seek its own level, one our adolescents can safely navigate.

THE CONTROL CONUNDRUM

WHETHER BECAUSE OF US OR IN SPITE OF US, OUR ADOLEScents have pledged allegiance to a new authority. While they do not question our power, they lay new claim to their own. So where does that leave us? We continue to guide not by sneaking or prying or even spying but by staying in sight, establishing boundaries, constantly reinforcing, and yielding the right-of-way whenever possible despite a relentless fear of the many temptations that mine their paths to self-discovery. We lead without fear of reprisal, follow without fear of rejection.

We also try to avoid the parenting trap that assumes that our bad childhood memories will become theirs, or that any bad ones of their own will cause permanent damage. We position ourselves as beacons worth following but don't expect them to remain close on our heels.

No one likes the feeling of being lost, in the dark, in a strange neighborhood, with no help in sight. Yet we've all been there, and found our way out, perhaps with varying degrees of success. So what do we want our adolescents to know, to think about when they find themselves adrift in a haze of indecision, unsure of which way to turn? Do we advise them to drop everything and wait for us to come to the rescue? Not very feasible. Not anymore. Like the infant finding the calm of her own thumb, don't we want their own voice of reason to calm any disabling qualms? Don't we want them to recognize where they've been so they can judge whether it makes more sense to turn back or forge ahead? Shouldn't our messages focus on how *they* must learn to operate their own internal dashboards because those are the only controls they can rely on when they're alone and in the sometimes slippery clutches of a choice? Isn't the lesson about how to measure the risks versus the rewards? Perhaps our best shot at control is training our adolescents to be their own protectorates. We may draw the boundaries for our adolescents but they, not us, must choose whether to remain within them.

Although we all make multiple mistakes, luckily, few of us are permanently disabled. But without the opportunity to make them, we might never learn which mistakes cause a stumble and which cause a fall. We might never learn to recognize our own reactions in the process—or how to pick ourselves back up and regroup. Few CEOs reflecting on their success diminish the value of learning from their failures. Yet relatively few of us would choose to add a safe opportunity to fail to our adolescent care packages.

> **US:** *Hi! Why so late getting home? Was the bus late today?*
> **THEM:** *No, actually, I took a later one cuz Kelly, Carla, and I went to The Bridge for a snack.*
> **US:** *Really? You mean you walked there from school? That's pretty far, isn't it?*
> **THEM:** *Well, we actually went with Miro Steinway. He's this really nice senior. He's really popular, and very responsible. We were just sitting around talking after classes and he offered. How many seniors do you know who would offer to take some freshmen out like that?*

*He's really cool and friendly, and he's a really good
driver.*
US: *I've heard you mention him before, but we've never
discussed you getting in a car with kids I don't know,
especially without discussing it with me first.*
THEM: *I know, I know, but you know what? I really
thought about it first and you've let me drive with Ayleen
and Kemp before so I really felt that you would put Miro
in the same category with them.*
US: *I might, but without talking about it with you, I can't
know. What if it had been someone else? Or different
circumstances?*
THEM: *That's what I mean, I wouldn't have gone! But
this guy is known as being the nicest and most responsible
guy in the entire school. It was one of those spur-of-the-
moment things and Kelly and Carla drive all the time
with their older brothers, so they knew their moms
wouldn't mind. And since you have let me drive with
responsible kids, and I am proving that I thought it
through, and I'm telling you now . . .*
US: *But what if his driving had made you feel unsafe?*

Clearly, the locus of control is shifting, and the thought
processes reflect reasonable, age-appropriate consideration.
All we can and need to do is to help it along by posing the
questions . . .

As unnatural as it sometimes feels, perhaps it is our turn
to allow *them* to push *us* to a new vantage point, where we
can peer over the brink of their vanishing childhoods into the
rushing rapids of adolescence. Rather than dragging them
kicking and screaming to our side of a dilemma, we expend
better energy by pointing out potential dangers and how to
avoid them.

Our job now is to help *them* learn how to stay safe. Some may need to learn the hard way.

US: *I couldn't help noticing those two girls talking with that group of boys over there. Do you know them?*

THEM: *Yeah, why?*

US: *Well, when they walked away, I could hear the boys saying things that weren't all that complimentary.*

THEM: *Like what?*

US: *Like "what a piece of ass" and "I'd like to get in her pants."*

THEM: *Guys say stuff like that all the time. They don't mean it as a cut. If anything, it's a compliment.*

US: *Do you think they're more apt to make those kinds of comments when girls wear clothes that show almost their entire bras or skirts that literally show the bottom of their butts?*

THEM: *No-oah!* [Sounds like *the ark owner.*] *That's just the way they dress! So you're saying girls can't dress the way they want? And if they choose to wear a short skirt, that makes them sluts?*

US: *Clothing should never turn the victim of sexual abuse into a perpetrator. I just worry about the message they're sending. To me, they seem to be more concerned about attracting attention to their bodies than to anything else. And it seems to be working. Do you see it differently?*

THEM: *Yeaaaah!* [Sounds like *duh.*] *They are just being themselves, and how they dress is up to them.*

US: *I understand what you're saying. But to me, everything we do, say, and in this case wear, sends a message. And we're the only ones who can control that.*

THEM: *Whatever . . .*

Therein lies the control conundrum. On the one hand, we try to resist the notion that our reign as benevolent dictators must change. On the other hand, we recognize that the only truly reliable outcome of imposed dominance is conflict. In the adolescent search for identity, we are either roadblocks or enablers. Put up a roadblock and we divert all their energy to getting around it. Better to put up a red flag and help them slow down long enough to consider the consequences.

> **US:** *I'm just not comfortable with your wearing those pants down by your thighs with half of your briefs exposed. I know you see it as your right, but it's mine to point out the hazards and set the limits. This is one of our limits. I know you don't agree, but we'll need to find some kind of solution.*
> **THEM:** *Geez, everyone does it, just look around! Why do you have to be so out of it?*
> **US:** *I know a lot of kids do, and that it makes you angry that we don't approve, but these are our limits; other parents have theirs. To us this is a matter of respect—not only toward us, but also toward others who don't want to have to read the labels on your underwear. So let's talk about an alternative . . .*

The sooner we recognize that we can no longer dictate to our adolescents, the better we can hone a much more effective parenting mechanism: motivation. For that, we rely on the Rules of Play.

> **THEM:** *Well, too bad; I'm wearing them. And you can't tell me what to do . . .*
> **US:** *You're right; I can't. Ultimately, it's your decision. But*

*I can tell you that if you do decide to wear that, then
you're not respecting the Rules of Play.*
THEM: *That's ridiculous! Why not?*
US: *Because you're not showing respect for what we
consider to be common decency. You know how we feel
about your underwear showing.* [Note the assumed
understanding of the ground rules.] *So it's up to you.
Just remember that if you decide to not abide by the Rules
of Play, you chip away at the foundation of trust and our
confidence in your choices. Remember, with freedom comes
responsibility, and showing responsibility buys you
freedom. It's your decision.*

While there may be a fuss, there shouldn't be any muss. It's
as simple as the Rules of Play.

A New Regime

WHAT HAPPENS WHEN, DESPITE A FIRM GRASP, LAYERS OF PRO-
tection, and careful steering on our parts, our adolescents
seem to float in a direction of their choosing, not ours?

What voices, words, and phrases accompany them when
the going gets tough and they are unsure which way to turn?
We hope, of course, that our adolescents recall the cautions
and wisdom we have inserted into countless faded conversations tattered by time. We hope that thousands of tiny morsels
of parental advice have simmered not as individual unwel-
comed warnings but as a stew of lasting impressions. We watch
for signs that our influence has infiltrated their internal conversations to which we are not privy but which we continue
to fund through a multitude of small contributions. These

conversations, begun as the audible but private role-plays of a toddler negotiating the imaginary perils of a nursery drama, have grown up. The adolescent voice we, and they, now hear speaks in many tongues, reflecting the guidance and advice from a mélange of authority figures, mentors, and peers—all part of their new internal-control regime.

> **US:** *Did you have fun last night?*
> **THEM:** *Yeah, it was all right.*
> **US:** [Our antennae up.] *What happened?*
> **THEM:** *Nothing.* [Knowing that *nothing* often means *something,* we tread lightly.]
> **US:** *You sound disappointed about something.*
> **THEM:** *Some kids were there.*
> **US:** *Were the parents?* [Still treading lightly.]
> **THEM:** *Yeah, but they were inside. They weren't really around.*
> **US:** *So what happened?*
> **THEM:** *I just hung with some kids. I sort of wish I hadn't even gone. It was stupid.*

And that may be it. That may be our one glimpse, this time, of their control mechanisms at work, their attempt to stay safe. An adolescent's control mechanisms lie deep within a conscience that we continue to nurture but did not create. It is *their* consciences, not ours, that conduct the ongoing debates between right and wrong, should and shouldn't; their commands, not ours, that maneuver them through so many internal skirmishes, most of which we never see or hear about. Often, we must simply settle for the laden *It was stupid,* or *I don't really care* as an indicator of a guarded but active resistance.

Staying in touch with our adolescents can take on many forms. It's up to us to be able to recognize them. One way to stay connected is to seek out ways to replenish their coping arsenals with enough fortification to fuel a multitude of internal debates.

> **US:** *Sounds like you handled the situation well. Next time you're worried about what might be happening if you go somewhere, why not invite some kids over here instead, or I could drop you all at a movie, or wherever.*

Control is no longer an option (for us) because our adolescents are able now to exercise their own. The better question might be—has it ever really been the option we thought it was?

TAKING THEIR TEMPERAMENTS

PRACTICALLY FROM BIRTH (IF NOT BEFORE), WE PUNCTUATE our communication with our children, both explicit and implicit, with control messages. We assume control as being more of a reflex than a learned behavior. A coveted ticket to acceptance in the outside world, our children's ability to demonstrate control is as much a display of our parenting abilities as of their emotional well-being. And (their) lack of it often constitutes grounds for public humiliation, if not punishment.

But unbeknownst even to them, our children have been sending us clearly marked handling instructions since day one. Whether on their first trip to the baby bath, or via countless everyday acts, their ability to be calmed, to adapt, to handle change, or to approach new things reveals a unique internal wiring, or temperament. These temperaments are the lenses through which our children view, and assert control over, their worlds. Most of our precious wonders arrive encased in one of three transparent, at least to them, temperaments: *easy, difficult,* and *slow-to-warm-up.*[1]

Woven into the fabric of our personalities with all the delicacy and imperfection of raw silk, temperaments, for better or for worse, predict the intensity of reactions, quality of moods, thresholds in the face of adversity, and persistence when surmounting obstacles. Like a fingerprint, our temperaments become our unique identifiers. Therefore, understanding our adolescents' temperaments, *as well as our own,* can often help to loosen the Gordian knot that binds many a parent-adolescent relationship.

Consider this scenario: A parent with an easy temperament readily adaptable to change, even-tempered and (usually) mellow, expects (at least initially) the offspring to go with the same flow. Instead, he or she finds an adolescent who sports a different—and difficult—temperament: The glass is always half empty; he or she radiates intensity; mulishly resists change. The resulting confrontations might go something like this:

> **THEM:** *Why can't I? You promised! Why do you always break your promises? You're such a hypocrite!*
> **US:** *Sweetie, why are you so upset? Calm down. It's not that big a deal!*
> **THEM:** *How would you know whether it's a big deal to me or not? Nothing is ever a big deal to you!*
> **US:** *C'mon now, no need to go on the attack. We can work this out.*
> **THEM:** *Yeah, right. That means do it your way! Look, this is important to me. I've been counting on it for weeks. You can't just change it just like that.*
> **US:** *It's not just like that. I warned you that this obligation might happen last week. Anyway, it's going to*

*be fun. You always blow things way out of proportion. Just
go with it. It'll be fun.*
THEM: *Why do you* always *say that?*

If that transcribes an easy-to-difficult (parent-to-adolescent) temperament conversation, imagine what two much more incompatible temperaments (say, difficult-to-difficult) might sound like:

THEM: *Why can't I? You promised! Why do you always
break your promises? You're such a hypocrite!*
US: *Now, hold on. Don't you dare talk to me like that!*
THEM: *Well, you lied to me! You said I could and now,
for no reason, you're going back on your word. That's lying.
Just like you always do!*
US: *That's it! I've had it with you . . .*

Given the risk of spontaneous combustion between two incompatible temperaments, it might be worth a little introspection in order to understand temperamental tendencies, both ours and theirs. Given the raw tinder of our adolescents' fragile emotions, we can't always prevent sparks from flying, but we can be aware of one possible source—us. Although control over our adolescents is no longer the point, control over *ourselves,* particularly our temperaments, must always be.

PLAYING WITH OUR ADOLESCENTS

WE MAY LOOK LIKE SENTINELS AT THE GATES OF OUR CHILDREN'S adolescence, arbitrating their activities, but in the end our adolescents execute *their* wills, not ours.

If we guard our adolescents with the weaponry of fear

and control, they will dedicate themselves to eluding our checkpoints and outsmarting our tactics (both of which they are very capable of doing). If we fail to guard them properly, they will seek protection elsewhere. But if we teach our adolescents the art of self-reliance, then they hone their instincts and look to us for both direction and backup. The first two tactics, fear and failure, either smother or neglect. The third tactic, self-reliance, shifts the locus of control to our adolescents and then gently but firmly holds them responsible for their actions. As parents, we may always have to deal, but we don't always have to prevail.

So if control is not the point, then what is? We know from our own experience that micromanagement can lead to such insidious relational viruses as deceit, disloyalty, and lack of communication. The best precaution against over- or undercontrol is the Rules of Play. But even the Rules of Play need to consist of the right balance of rules and play. In fact, sometimes our most successful alternatives to control involve playfulness.

Let's imagine actually being included, as opposed to feeling excluded, in the adolescent party. Not as a friend, or a guest, or even the host, but as a permanent participant in a multigenerational gathering. Like any good party, the adolescent one buzzes with the expected titillations and complexities. And the best way to garner a coveted invitation is to be good company.

In the company of our adolescents, we neither hover nor impose, but mingle, not self-consciously but consciously observing. Mostly we enjoy. Like any good conversationalist, we try to focus on our adolescents' accomplishments as a way of drawing them out. Though we still wear the telltale whistle of authority around our necks, we reserve it for emergencies. At times, our adolescents might even regard these whistles as slightly reassuring, though they would never say so.

So appreciative are we to be included, we recall where we stashed some remnants of our own adolescent playfulness. Maybe it's the freshness of their humor, or the raw innocence with which they enthuse about everything and nothing, that motivates us to respond in kind. For there are some games it's okay to play with our adolescents—and still be respectable parents, and respected as parents. Think of these games as strategies for keeping in touch, alternative ways of weighing in, rather than weighing down. Think of levity as a kind of diplomacy that prevents tensions from escalating out of control.

GAMES IT'S OKAY TO PLAY

THE KEY TO THESE STRATEGIES IS THEIR INCREDIBLE LIGHTness of being. Do we risk striking out sometimes? Yes. We're not looking for home runs, just a few singles. The whole point is to stay in *their* game. If we're not, we can't know what's going on. Here are a few more lighthearted methods we might try in order to stay in touch.

1. The *It's a Wonderful Day in the Neighborhood* Game

Usually a closed door sends a pretty clear message. Although the need for privacy is a hallmark of adolescence, it needn't be taken as a desire, or a right, to exclude. The best way to shut ourselves off from our adolescents is to keep *ourselves* out. Every closed adolescent door opens onto a room, a room in *our* home that also belongs to *them*. If we want access, we need only knock to signal our visit (unless we are *truly* worried about their safety and welfare—in which case, we enter regardless). No response? That's okay; we were in the neighborhood and thought we'd stop in for a quick visit. Surprised to see us invite ourselves in, just like that? Respond simply by finding an open space on a chair or on the floor. Maybe just plonk down on the bed. Most important, be comfortable, as if we belong (which we do, we're their parents). Be cheerful, as if we're happy to see them (which we are, they're our kids, and this won't be their dedicated hideout for that much longer). No agenda or small talk needed. Even bring a book or the newspaper. It's a wonderful day in the neighborhood, just stopped in for a visit. Stay for a few minutes, or longer. Sense the mood. If it's unwelcoming, add some warmth: *I was in the neighborhood and missed you. Thought I'd stop in.* If there's music playing, ask who it is (and mean it). Timing is everything; so are the little connections. Once made, they get easier. Next time, they won't be as surprised, though they still might repel us or throw some verbal darts. Pretty soon, a twinge of welcome might even flash across their rolling eyes. Keep it light but sincere. Keep it regular. Just like Mr. Rogers.

2. The *Catch Them Off-Guard* Game

Related to the *It's a Wonderful Day in the Neighborhood* game, this one hinges on the element of surprise. Lest they think they've got our number, don't be afraid to try a new one. Bar none, parenting is the most creative job we'll ever have. Creativity actually nourishes incentive to change a behavior much more effectively than penalties do. Like laughter, creativity can be disarming, especially if accompanied by spontaneity. Best of all, creativity rarely causes any contraindications.

Here are some ways to play the *Catch Them Off-Guard* game:

■ **Reward, don't punish, most attempts to finesse us.**

THEM: *I knew you'd be angry about my grades this term, but I've met with my teachers and worked out some ways to get extra credit, and finish my paper . . .*

In other words, give (extra) credit for trying.

US: *You're right, I'm not thrilled with these grades. So right now, I'm more interested in your plans to improve them. I'm willing to listen, as long as I see results.*

Anticipating and presenting the right data is a critical life skill.

■ **Convey disapproval with humor.** When possible, it's okay to conceal anger with humor. Just look at most political cartoonists.

Are they spending too much time on the computer, despite repeated admonitions? Sit or stand right next to them, up close and personal, like a shadow. Let them feel the heat of our presence but not our anger. They know the limit, and when it's been crossed. If they try to close the door on us, literally or figuratively, open it. Say nothing. Don't get mad, get close.

Still too much time on the computer, despite lengthy discussion and a bipartisan agreement on the definition of "too much"? As the systems administrators of our households (assuming we pay the Internet bill), a range of options exist. Devices abound to observe, limit and even block Internet meanderings. And even the Luddites among us should know how to unplug a router or stow a cable for an Internet "time-out." When withdrawal hits, it may be time for a cookies and milk break, ready and waiting. And more discussion.

THEM: *You can't just stop the Internet! I have homework to do!*
US: *[Smile. Remember the humor.] Sure I can. As the systems administrator of this family, if a system is being abused, we have to work on it. So let's do that . . .*

Note: Even though many of today's teenagers can easily resort to their Smartphones for temporary relief from an Internet drought, the point will still be made. Calm creativity—guaranteed to spice up a little humor.

■ **Invoke the silly clause (best done in the privacy of close friends and family).** We all know how; we just sometimes forget, or prefer not to open ourselves up to the ridicule. A funny bone doesn't go away, it's just that age or fatigue or even scar tissue sometimes obfuscates it. And just because they don't "lol" doesn't mean they aren't amused—or they want us to stop. Lol'ing at the wrong people (or things) can be viewed (by them) as a serious infraction. But they will almost always laugh at us laughing at ourselves. There is no better medicine for the adolescent that ails us than humor.

3. The *Last Word* Game

This one moves out of the humor realm into more of a correctional one. As their prefrontal cortex vies for control over a raging limbic system (see chapter 1, Their Brains Are to Blame), we often find ourselves in the crosshairs of some verbal sharpshooting. Curiously, we are often aiming at the same targets they are—namely, the need to be right, and the desire to get our way. Hence the onset of a frustratingly circular contest, the effect of which can be dizzying.

It's time to play . . . the *Last Word* game! Here are the rules: As soon as we recognize a downward-spiraling conversation, we need only take one baby step to the side in order to free ourselves from its clutches. In doing so, we remove ourselves from the entire competition.

> **THEM:** *I told you: I'm tired, I have a lot of homework and I don't want to go.*
> **US:** *This is a family event. You've known about it for weeks. It won't kill you to go.*
> **THEM:** *Yes it will!*
> **US:** *Sorry [and mean it], I know you don't want to go, but this is nonnegotiable.*
> **THEM:** *Well, I'm not going.*
> **US:** *Okay, now we're playing the* Last Word *game, which, as you know, is one of my least favorites.*

Step one: name it.

> **US:** *We're leaving in thirty minutes. We really want you to come. If you choose not to now, there will be consequences because we had an understanding [If inclined, refer to the Show Respect Rule of Play as a rationale.]*

Step two: remind them that bad decisions lead to consequences.

> **THEM:** *Well, I'm not going.*
> **US:** *Sounds like that's the last word.*

Step three: declare it over, even while letting them have the last word (which they invariably will), if not the last thought. (Knowing what to expect frees us to ignore it.) Then comes the really creative part: inventing a consequence. [For some suggestions, see chapter 2, Truth Is as Malleable . . .]

Here's another version of the *Last Word* game.

> **US:** *I've been listening to you two bicker for twenty minutes and now it's preventing me from getting my work done.*
> **THEM 1:** *It's his fault. He started it. I was here first.*
> **THEM 2:** *You were not! I was here first. Anyway, you said you were done.*
> **THEM 1:** *I did not!*
> **THEM 2:** *Well, I'm not getting off . . .*

Assuming we have more than one child, we've probably gotten ensnared by similar sibling uprisings. Before we get to the end of our rope, or they hang each other with theirs, we try:

> **US:** *Hold on! Sounds to me like we're playing the Last Word game, which, as you know, is one of my least favorites.*

Step one: name it.

> **US:** *You two can't seem to work this out. I can't live with the bickering. So, here's the deal. You two need to figure out how to share this. That was the understanding when we got it and I expect you both to respect that [*Show Respect Rule of Play*]. If you can't, then I'll have to come up with a solution—which you might not like very much . . .*

Step two: warn that bad decisions carry ramifications, but refrain (just yet) from issuing one.

> **THEM 1:** *Well, it's not my fault, so I shouldn't have to do anything.*

> **THEM 2:** *Well, it's not my fault. You started it.*
> **US:** *Sounds like that's the last word on the subject.*

Step three: declare the disagreement over, which it won't be, precisely because they haven't had the last word yet—with each other, or with us.

> **THEM 1:** *Yep. You're right and I'm wrong. As usual.* [Or some such *Last Word* game–type statement.]

Say nothing. *Let* them have the last word. It's by far the shortest route to a good point. By then, if the situation hasn't resolved itself, our only task is to produce a creative solution (which hopefully involves leaving them to work it out—a little more quietly). And that is the last word.

Note: A word about attitude. Attitude darts that have nowhere to land usually aren't worth shooting. By declaring the competition for the last word over, we may open ourselves up as a target for a last barb or two, but then we move on, effectively removing ourselves as a target. Because most adolescents focus on getting *what* they want *when* they want it, they usually limit their aggression to current battles (and targets). We capitalize on this predisposition by letting bygones (and attitude) be bygones and move on to another topic.

> **US:** *I'm so glad you found your lost sneaker. Where did you say it was?*

4. The *Name That Tune* Game

A variation on the *Last Word* game, this one offers another way to turn off the adolescent polemics vacuum that chases after us with a relentless sucking motion.

THEM: *I wasn't being rude. You're just not listening.*
US: *I am listening. You just don't like what I'm saying.*
THEM: *Well, then why can't I?*
US: *I've already answered that question.*
THEM: *No, you haven't. Give me one good reason.*

It's time to play . . . *Name That Tune.*

US: *I understand that you're angry because you're not getting what you want.*

Step one: recognize the rapidly derailing conversation. Step two: name the behavior.

US: *I would be angry, too, if I were in your shoes. But now I'm getting angry, so I'm going to end this conversation and go finish my work [or whatever]. We can discuss it more later if there's something new to add. We've each expressed our opinions, so now I need to get off this particular merry-go-round . . .*
THEM: *But why can't you give me a reason? I just need one good reason!*
US: *I've given you several; you just don't like them. But that doesn't change them.*

Step three: we give them the benefit of the doubt (but only if we can do so calmly) in case they didn't hear it the first time by playing *Name That Tune*—again. If that doesn't work, revert to the *Last Word* game. (Step one: name the game, [i.e., the *Last Word* game]; Step two: warn that bad decisions carry ramifications, but refrain from issuing a specific consequence;

Step three: declare the game over, but assume one last word from them.)

Or we resort to step four: create a solution or consequence, only if necessary.

Remember, the success of all these games hinges on our ability to change the pace of a deteriorating situation without losing contact. Our connection to our adolescents doesn't always need to be on; it just needs to be working.

5. The *Afterthought* Game

Why do our best responses, or questions, always seem to occur to us later, out of range from the moment but still under its influence? Don't despair; it's never too late. A kind of parenting antacid, the *Afterthought* game eases the distress of an unresolved situation. The skilled participant forgoes the urge to stuff centuries' worth of wisdom into a single discussion, lest his or her moral gets buried. Lastly, the *Afterthought* game spares us from one of parenting's worst humiliations: to be rendered speechless. Or one of parenting's worst tendencies: lack of follow-through.

Here are the rules. Step one: start with the *It's a Wonderful Day in the Neighborhood* game. Step two: immediately launch into the *Catch Them Off-Guard* game:

> **US:** *You know I was thinking about our discussion the other day and I wanted to ask you . . . [Or, I've been thinking about a good consequence for that situation the other day, and here's what I've decided . . .]*

With hindsight as our ally, we try again.

HOW TO DEAL

1. Focus on the process, not the endpoint.

2. Anticipate, anticipate, anticipate (because they can't).

3. Think about the voice, words, and message you want them to replay.

4. Know our rights—and theirs.

5. Be ready and able to disengage at any moment.

---

1. Focus on the Process, Not the Endpoint

If things run amok, we remain focused on honing our teenagers' controls, not exercising ours. Whether performing routine maintenance or responding to an emergency, we employ a rigorous troubleshooting process with our adolescents that relies on a constantly updated and strategic question set. Using the 3 D's—*dispassion, distance,* and *dispensation*—we plumb for information. Conduct an inquisition and we turn our adolescents into defendants; include them in the collaboration and we join forces.

> **US:** *What made you decide to stay at the party even when you knew there was stuff going on? Did you figure that you could stay safe despite the fact that there was drinking and pot?* [Try to gain entrance to their internal conversation; they have no interest in ours.]

THEM: *Yeah, I guess.*
US: *What would you have done if the police had shown up?*
THEM: *They didn't, so stop worrying.*
US: *If they had? What would you have done?*
THEM: *I don't know. It depends.*
US: *Seriously, do you know what could have happened if they had?*
THEM: *I suppose. But you always harp on that and it never happens.*

At every available opportunity, call in the data forces. Keep a record (either mentally or, better yet, clipped from the headlines) of as many stories as possible that elucidate the ramifications of bad adolescent judgment—the closer to home and more horrific, the better. Let the data do the talking. Our job is not to corner or trap, it's to prepare them, which sometimes requires scare tactics.

US: *Remember what happened to the Anderson kids: suspended from school, a night in jail, followed by a court appearance with a pretty nasty judge and a year of community service. That's every weekend for a whole year! They could easily have gotten slapped with a criminal record, too.*
THEM: *Mr. Anderson's a lawyer; he would never have let that happen.*
US: *He may be a lawyer, but that's no insurance against a tough judge. The only things you can truly count on from us are love, support, and forgiveness. We can't bend the law and we won't, even if we could [*because we know the message it would send*]. At this point, you are much more in control of your life than we are.*

Even the gravest of questions, asked with dispassion, remain at a safe distance. And generous fairness with our dispensations lets us generously reward the truth.

> **US:** *So what was your plan?*
> **TRANSLATION:** *Tell me a little bit about your thought process.*

If they say they didn't have one, that's informative. We seize any opportunity to role-play, and dog-ear useful scripts for an unanticipated future.

The endpoint of a situation usually isn't reversible, whether it's a missed curfew, a bad grade, or some other outcome. But the process, or decision, leading to the endpoint will likely repeat itself over and over. Given our adolescents' inability to anticipate effectively on a consistent basis, in part a function of incomplete brain development, we constantly help mark the best route to a decision by posing questions, risks, and alternatives for them to consider. The sooner our adolescents recognize that there is more than one route to a decision, the better they will learn to weigh different options. And the more they retrace their decision-making footsteps, the more familiar those steps become. This is how the adolescent brain learns to make consistently sound choices (see chapter 1, Their Brains Are to Blame).

Not all of our questions need to focus on *them*. In fact, questioning them about *our* performance exposes enough of our own vulnerability to keep them, and us, honest. Recalling the mantra from chapter 2 (Truth Is as Malleable . . .), wouldn't it be nice occasionally to hear their honest thoughts free of charge or accusation, regarding our performance? Some tactics for soliciting feedback might include:

- *Did I screw up there?*
- *Are you angry with me?*
- *Do you think I'm disappointed in you a lot?*
- *Do you feel like we put a lot of pressure on you?*
- *If you could change one thing about us, what would it be?*

Most of us don't hesitate to dish out honest feedback; shouldn't we be able to take some, too?

2. Anticipate, Anticipate, Anticipate (Because They Can't)

Even though they must win their own battle for control, we know the enemies better than they do. Perhaps our biggest advantage in the control struggle is the fact that most adolescents (*and* adults) never fully wean from the need for parental approval. In some ironic twist of development, we help to nourish the fertile soils of the impulsive adolescent limbic system, which can sprout some pretty exotic varieties of narcissism. But at least we now understand that such growth comes with the adolescent territory.

> **THEM:** *. . . So that's the plan; I've got it all worked out, you don't need to worry about any of the driving.*
> **US:** *Well, you certainly have all the bases covered, but I'm not sure why it needs to be so elaborate. I'm happy to pick you and any friends up. It's not at all inconvenient.*

First warning sign: unnecessarily complicated plans.

> **THEM:** *No, no, really. It's okay. This is the only way it works for everybody. Honestly, we worked really hard on this and it's all set. Really, I'm serious.*

Second warning sign: the babble barometer keeps rising. Remembering the three D's, dispassion, distance, and dispensation, we couch our questions in a comfortable nonchalance.

> **US:** *Tell me again why you need to make so many stops before getting to Rory's house?*
> **THEM:** *Just because everyone's schedule is so different, and Marny has to work till six and Reilly's mom is away and . . .*
> **US:** *Listen, I'd feel better if I spoke to Rory's mom or dad. Maybe I can help out somehow. I think I'll give them a call.*
> **THEM:** *No! No! Really, we've got it all settled. C'mon, you don't need to check up on me every time I make a plan. Anyway, you always say, "Present me a plan and then I'll decide." Well, here it is! And I promise to call if anything changes. So what's the problem?*

Third warning sign: outrage! The higher the voltage, the greater the likelihood of a shortage of reasoning.

> **US:** *I can see you've worked hard on this and you really want it to work. I can also see that my resistance is making you quite upset [the Name That Tune game]. But it's my job to anticipate any problems, and to be honest I have some concerns. It feels overly complicated, so I'm worried that I'm missing something. Am I?*
> **THEM:** *No! I told you, I've got it all worked out.*
> **US:** *Okay. I would just feel better chatting with Rory's mom or dad. Or any other parent who is involved in the plan. It doesn't matter who. Which way would you like me to go?*

We anticipate by listening and questioning with distance and dispassion, stakes in the ground that always mark the high

road. Distance allows us to set limits and impose consequences based on the three simple Rules of Play that we've all
agreed to: stay safe, show respect, keep in touch. Dispassion
lets the Rules of Play do the talking. Dispensation gives our
teenagers a chance to work things out on their own—and
again if they need to.

3. Think About the Voice, Words, and Message You Want Them to Replay

Would we even know if our adolescents were stranded on the
corner of a decision, unsure which way to turn because of too
many choices or stresses, or too few? When standing on the
brink of any decision, most of us use similar tactics: We weigh
the options hoping that some permutation or combination
will push us to the tipping point. How we get there and the
amount of force needed to unbalance the scales differs for
each of us. The same holds true for our ability to influence
our adolescents. *How* we say what we say can carry as much
weight as the words themselves.

Old news to many of us: Our parenting styles generally
fall into one of three categories: *authoritarian, permissive,* or *authoritative.* These styles form the often unconscious stances
we take when communicating with our adolescents. Ever
wonder how these parenting styles inform our adolescents'
thought processes? What most of us would give to eavesdrop
on those precious, behavior-inducing internal conversations.
Let's conjecture.

> ■ **The adolescent of authoritarian parents might
> think . . .** *If I ask, they'll say no without even hearing me
> out and if I get caught [not if I do it], my reasons won't
> matter, they'll just let me have it anyway. So given how*

important this is to me, I need to figure out a way around them . . .

■ **The adolescent of permissive parents might think . . .** *I can usually talk them into it, especially if I tell them everybody else is doing it. And anyway, what's the worst that can happen? It backfires and they have to help me figure out how to get out of it. That's what they're there for, isn't it?*

■ **The adolescent of authoritative parents might think . . .** *I know what they'll be concerned about, so I need to figure out how to handle those concerns. They trusted me the last time even though it was a smaller deal, so I just need to convince them that I can handle this and not screw up. If they give me flak, I'll tell them I'll stay in the next two weekends and do whatever else they want. I've earned this by being responsible, now they have to live up to their end by trusting me . . .*

Authoritarian parents truly believe they own the mechanisms of control, while authoritative parents merely manage them. Permissive parents often opt to relinquish control entirely, which places adolescents under the jurisdiction of their own inadequate judgment.

Awareness of our prevailing parenting style allows us to reflect on our own favorite techniques, such as questions, meaningful examples, best practices, reasonable consequences, and so on, to make sure that we are doing everything we can to keep the conversation going.

4. Know Our Rights—and Theirs

Before yanking the reins of control, we need to ask who the cinching action will benefit. Not sure? Then here's a test: When an adolescent seeks permission for something, is our first reaction usually *no*? If so, then our need to demonstrate control may end up drowning out some developmentally crucial conversations with our adolescents. If our default is set on *no,* then we had better be versatile at deciphering elaborate adolescent codes and adept at playing cat and mouse. On the other hand, if our first reaction is *If you can show me how you're going to do this* [whatever *this* is] *while abiding by the Rules of Play,* then we have lots to talk about.

If asked, most revered teachers rank the opportunity to keep learning, not just from books or colleagues, but also from students, high on their list of motivators. How many *learnable* moments do *we* overlook in our search for the teachable ones? Since our adolescents can often see things from angles we cannot, what may appear to us as unessential, or inconsequential, to them is an unassailable right—or the truth. When we hear a strain from Beethoven's Ninth Symphony embedded into a cacophonous rap tune, we often decry it as ripped off or bastardized. Our adolescents praise the originality and creativity. Which is it?

> **US:** *But honey, are you sure you want to quit now? You've put so many years into this, and you're really good at it. Why stop now?*
> **THEM:** *Because I've thought about it a lot and I just can't do it anymore plus get my schoolwork done plus do the other things I want to do. Something has to go and this is what I've chosen.*
> **US:** *I know you have a lot on your plate, but you have a talent that could really help you down the road, like when you apply to college. We've invested a lot of money in this and we just can't let you quit now.*

Whose decision is this, anyway? Do we really want to let years of investment go to waste? After all, we're their parents and therefore know better. When do our rights become wrong? Probably when they can recognize a good decision (for them) better than we can. Here's an alternative response:

> **US:** *I know you have a lot on your plate; but you have a talent that could really help you down the road, like when you apply to college. If you want to try to stick with it, let's see if there's anything we can do to help you juggle everything.*
> **THEM:** *But I've really tried to do that. I've talked with Coach and my teachers. I just think that if I concentrate on fewer things, I can do better in those things instead of always feeling like I'm behind.*
> **US:** *Then it's sounds like you've set your priorities, which is a really hard thing to do. We'll support whatever you decide.*

Simply adjusting the tautness of the reins of control (being careful not to wrench nor let go entirely) can lend a different tone to the adult–adolescent conversation.

5. Be Ready and Able to Disengage at Any Moment

As difficult as disengaging is for most of us, it is even more so for an adolescent. Although we can't control their actions, we can control our impulse to retaliate, knowing that in the end we wield much more potential to inflict harm than do they. Think of our adolescents as a work in progress. That's their excuse. We have none. When it comes to showing respect, we cannot ask for what we do not give.

Most of us are natural referees, accustomed to calling fouls as we see them. During our children's adolescence, however, we are much more needed, and effective, as coaches:

clear on the rules, watching out for their safety, keeping our teenagers focused on the right goals. By far our best game plan reflects the fact that most of our adolescents genuinely want to please us. By far our most effective response to their many small mistakes is a reasoned display of disappointment.

US: *What were you working on at the computer for so long?*
THEM: *Nothing, just homework.* [Again, aware that *nothing* usually means *something,* we probe—gently.]
US: *Are you finished?*
THEM: *No, not quite.* [We know from their working style that an entire term paper could have been written in that time slot. So, if the air is clear enough, consider adding: *I read an article recently that explained that the brain can't actually process more than one thing at a time so the more time you spend chatting, the longer your homework will take.*]
US: *From the sound of your fingers flying across the keys, I could have sworn there was a chat of some sort going on in there somewhere.*
THEM: *You weren't even in the room, how do you know what I was doing?*
US: *I don't, which is why I have to trust you to hold up your end of the agreement to make sure all your homework is finished before any chatting, texting, Facebooking, or whatever.*
TRANSLATION: *I'm wiser than you think (or fear). I know I can't know everything that is going on. But I still expect you to hear my voice in your head and to abide by our agreements. Will I bust you for every offense? No. Do I trust you to get your work done and maintain the grades*

we agreed on? Yes. If you betray my trust, then we
reevaluate—and you face the consequences. If I betray your
trust, then our grounds for negotiating crumble, because
without your trust, I know you will choose the path
around, rather than through, me.

An even trade? Not necessarily. A fair trade? Yes, because raising an adolescent is not a contest. There are no winners or losers; there's just the hope that we all make it through safely, with mutual respect—and more to talk about.

US: *I'd be really disappointed if you were on Facebook or texting and couldn't admit it. That's more important to me than anything else.*

Using a variety of conversational devices (poetic, dramatic, humorous, what have you), we reinforce the three Rules of Play over and over again. No matter how far off-course we may drift in the midst of an adolescent conversation, we rely on the Rules of Play to return us to the core concepts of safety, respect, communication. The Rules of Play remain our best way to stay engaged—and our best method to disengage when we need to. And so goes the parenting balancing act. It's the ongoing conversations with our adolescents that keep us level.

COMMAND OF CONTROL

BY ADOLESCENCE, *THEY* ARE THE ONLY ONES WHO CAN ACCU-rately make the baseline calls. That used to be us, but not any-more. So we must rely on their inner voice—the voice that musters the real *no* when faced with temptation. The voice that stands up to an injustice. The voice that calls in to report a changed plan. The voice that senses danger and how to avoid it, that abides by the three Rules of Play. Only when we hear that voice are we assured that the only truly *reliable* mechanisms of control are at work: theirs. That is the voice we listen for—and answer. That is the voice we bolster and enforce. That is the voice on its way to adulthood.

As if belaying their life's ropes as they ascend the heights of adolescence, we release freedom when they earn it, curtail it when they don't. The higher our adolescents climb, the more distant their nods back to us. Are they saying something or just signaling that they're okay? Unsure, we keep watch. Sometimes, only luck prevents a fall; other times, they scurry up the steepest of slopes, sure-footed and agile. After all, it is their adolescence to scale; we only point out the secure footholds. Perhaps the control we most fear losing is over the connection that draws them to our bedside to say good night (since by adolescence our bedtime often precedes theirs), or causes them to linger an extra moment at the table—just to talk. Perhaps the control we most seek is not control at all. It is simply a longing for a conversation just between us two. The kind that often takes place late at night where the light only shines on the parts of us that are the same.

THE ADOLESCENT MIRROR DISTORTS

AWARENESS OF THE POWER OF THE ADOLESCENT MIRROR IS less important than an awareness of where its distortions can lead. The reflections our teenagers see provide instantaneous feedback as tactlessly and irrefutably as a bathroom scale. Each glimpse offers another opportunity for inspection; each inspection invites the possibility of rejection by either the adolescent self or, worse, others. A sort of metaphysical diary, the adolescent mirror (what *they* see and, therefore, what they think *others* see) both knows all and conveys little about the true disposition of its informants. Though the adolescent mirror may not lie, it can certainly distort an adolescent's search for self.

> **US:** *Your hair looks fine, but take another look in the mirror and make sure you really want to wear that much eye makeup.*
> **THEM:** *What are you talking about? I hardly put any on! But I hate my hair; it's sooo ugly!*

The statistics concerning the prevalence of adolescent depression and suicide are hard to even think about, let alone accept. No matter how well we distance or insulate ourselves from such realities, these statistics invariably reflect a family next door or from the next grade.

Research shows that 8 percent of twelve- to seventeen-year-olds suffer from major depression, and those who have are at greater risk for suicide as well as substance abuse.[1] Almost 15 percent of adolescents seriously consider suicide, and 7 percent will actually attempt it before age nineteen, males four times more often than females.[2] Each year, more than ten thousand attempts are successful, making it the third leading cause of death among fifteen- to twenty-four-year-olds.[3] Although the most recent studies show a slight decline, actual suicide rates for adolescents have tripled over the last thirty years.[4] Shocking, but should it be?

We have all experienced feelings of futility or gloom. But in an adolescent, these depressive feelings can slowly decay even the most carefully constructed shields of makeup, clothing, or affect. For many, the feelings settle in as manageable self-doubt. For others, the erosion continues, seriously impairing natural self-help mechanisms such as hope and motivation. Hard to describe and harder to shed, some form of melancholy haunts most adolescents, staring back at them from every mirror, following them into every room, spotlighting every imperfection.

> **US:** *This is the fifth time you've changed your outfit. What was wrong with the first one?*
> **THEM:** *It made me look fat. I hated it.*

WHAT WE SEE IS NOT WHAT WE GET

TEASED INTO BELIEVING (BY ADULT-DRIVEN MEDIA AND OTHER influences) that perfection need only be skin-deep, adolescents lack the cognitive, emotional, and social ability to find a comfortable, let alone perfect, self-image. The average person receives four hundred to six hundred commercial messages per day. One out of ten relates to body image.[5] Add that to the number of times our adolescents compare themselves to members of their own peer group, whether in the classroom, online, in the locker room, or merely walking down the hallway. Each comparison, conducted with the ease and accuracy of a bar code scan, matches up input from dozens of data points, ranging from hair and physique to academic and athletic prowess. Any mismatches highlight the most flagrant flaws, naked and raw for all to see.

Adolescents are the most marketed-to population group in history.[6] And their hyperfocus on the internal is redefining the media and marketing assault on the American consumer. If that is not surprising, what may be is the fact that the ubiquitous marketing tentacles that squeeze the individuality out of our adolescents' self-image belong primarily to the top four megaconglomerates, namely, Disney, News Corporation, Viacom, and Time Warner.[7] By hook or by (psychological) crook, these powerhouses dictate the buying habits of an eager and impressionable wannabe market of thirty-two million adolescents to the tune of an expected $208 billion per year by 2011 (an increase of more than 50 billion over the last ten years). This despite a 3 percent decline in the twelve- to seventeen-year-old population.[8] (If it's any consolation, teen spending money comes to about 91 billion; the rest we spend on their behalf, even though the annual incomes of 80 percent of us is less than $75,000.)[9, 10] Employing a tactic called "cool hunting," these media tastemakers titillate our adolescents into buying submission not just year after year, but season after season. Think about the clothes they wear (or *must* have), the movies they watch (or *must* see), the food they eat (or would eat *24/7* if they could), the gadgets they need, the stars or athletes they idolize, the magazines they read, the phraseology they use, the music that bombards their airwaves (not to mention the lyrics), and the behaviors they normalize as a result. Think about the time they spend social networking; playing computer games, spending those hundreds of billions per year. The deeper our adolescents wade into the vast and inviting Internet waters, the wider the new media marketing trawlers cast their nets for teen-purchasing attention.

In many ways, these four companies, and all that they convey, represent the stiffest competition for our adolescents' attention. But unfortunately, it's not that simple. After all, aren't we the generation responsible for, if not creating then certainly inflating, this marketing megamonster? And even if we don't count ourselves among its creators, we all help sustain this media-inspired societal ecosystem. How many of us confess to sneaking a peek at an idle *National Enquirer* or being snared by a fashion trend or singing along with a top pop tune filtering through the grocery store airwaves? Even a two-year-old can identify with the lyrics, "Tonight's gonna be a good, good night . . . just take it off . . . just do it, do it, do it . . ."[11] but how many of us stop to analyze these words, let alone confront their implication? And what if we did? Isn't this an example of the harmless, if ubiquitous, ear candy that we may not like but cannot avoid? Probably not many of us can name the brand of underwear worn by the quarterback of last year's winning Super Bowl team. But we might be surprised by how many of our adolescents can. And for many, knowing is wanting.

The adolescent search for identity has always been fueled by comparisons, even unfair or contrived ones. For many, the search can lead to borrowing or, worse, stealing from others (either literally, as in clothing or money, or figuratively, as in rumors or backstabbing) as a way to prop up inferiorities. (One study reported that 38 percent of the twelve thousand adolescents surveyed admitted to stealing from a store within the last year.)[12] The desire to achieve perfection is a hunger that can never be satisfied. Ever hopeful, adolescents carry a long list of "if onlys" that if only they had, didn't have, or could get, all would be well. If only the walls of loneliness were transparent, our adolescents might be surprised at how many of their peers they would recognize.

What They See Is Not What We See

WHILE OUR ADOLESCENTS SEE THEIR REFLECTIONS FROM THE inside looking out, we see *them* from the outside and try to look in. Where we see a pimple as a temporary surface wound merely grazing a much more existential and lasting beauty, they see it as a flesh-eating vermin invading innocent pores, plotting its next attack. Reflexively, we focus on fixing any flaws; they focus on covering them up, lest anyone expose the turmoil inside. Where we see that crisp new shirt or adorable top, they see a curve or crimp or bulge guaranteed to draw sneers from anyone with eyes. Unable to read normal cues accurately, especially ours, adolescents automatically assign every word, look, and gesture aimed in their direction to the criticism column, where it is easily misread or misunderstood, triggering a defensive response (often unleashed as aggression). Thus goes the tale of the distorted adolescent mirror.

It's not so much the distortions themselves, for they have withstood the test of time, but the intensity of the adolescent response that need concern us. So we increase our surveillance of some of their more sensitive or concealed reactions, such as their ability to rebound from a bad grade or a breakup with a friend (same or opposite gender) or their ability to regain perspective after a fight with a sibling—or us.

> **US:** *I know you really cared about Lina and really miss being with her. When you were together, what was the best part?*
> **THEM:** *I don't know . . . she was just fun to be around.*
> **US:** *Was that the most important part for you? What wasn't good?*
> **THEM:** *I guess never knowing how she really felt. The not knowing . . .*
> **US:** *Sounds like you expected, or maybe wanted, that to be different?*
> **THEM:** *I guess I wished it was . . .*

We model coping, with or without an answer or solution, so that our adolescents learn to cope on their own. We help soothe the raw emotions that symptomize myriad adolescent traumas by helping them analyze and dissect (a natural instinct for most adolescents) what happened. They have no idea what lies ahead; we at least have some. Maybe we can help them be ready, even if we weren't.

And sometimes, we need a little coping assistance ourselves. Often, a little stimulation of the compassion glands is all it takes. One quick way to revisit the nagging ache of rejection or the insatiable need for reinforcement is to recall some of the distorted images from our own adolescence. Remember walking into a room full of people, most of whom were not even aware of our presence, and feeling the intense magnification of every hair out of place, every awkward gesture? Or conjure an image of being dogged by a revolving jury of peers, parents, teachers, and coaches, all rendering their own opinions and verdicts.

US: *Good job, honey, you were great!*
THEM: *I was not, didn't you see me screw up? I can't believe I did that . . .*
US: *What do you mean? No one noticed anything . . .*
THEM: *Are you kidding? I screwed up all over the place. Why do you always say I was great when you know it's not true?*

We resist ringing the defense alarm: *I do not! If you had screwed up, I'd tell you! Don't be so hard on yourself. Everyone thinks you're great!* Or even the disappointment alarm: *It makes me feel really bad when you accuse me of something that I didn't do. I really don't think you're being fair with me on this.*

Instead, we could stick to our job, in this case to help them find and maintain their balance, especially when they're off-kilter.

US: *I'm sorry if I upset you. That wasn't my intention at all. I guess we just see things differently on this. Tell me how I can make you feel better?*
THEM: *Oh, forget it.*

And we do. Until the next time one of our idle comments on its way to a compliment gets rerouted to a criticism. Then we try again.

THE ONLY ADOLESCENT PERSPECTIVE—THEIR OWN

NOT ONLY DO ADOLESCENTS LACK THE CAPACITY TO REFLECT on their own decisions, but they are also unable to reconcile the differences between their imagined selves and their real selves. No wonder our reassurances frequently don't ring true. Often our most heartfelt, best-meant reinforcements—*Don't worry, honey, I think you're beautiful*—carry less credibility than a fortune cookie platitude. How could we not see that if only they had different hair, weight, clothes, equipment, grades, they'd surely win today's adolescent challenge? Secure in our own possession of an identity, we easily forget the discomfort of not having one firmly in our grasp.

So the next time we lament or lambaste an adolescent act of random disregard or insensitivity, we remember how difficult it is to recognize the needs of others when their view of themselves is so out of focus.

> **US:** *You look kinda glum. Bad day today?*
> **THEM:** *Yeah, I guess.*
> **US:** *What happened?*
> **THEM:** *Not much.*
> **US:** *Like what?*

Again, we tread lightly, testing whether the curtness is penetrable. They'll let us know.

> **THEM:** *Just a little fight with Tandy.*
> **US:** *Oh dear. Were you two able to work it out?*
> **THEM:** *I think so. We'll see.*
> **US:** *Don't you want to hear about Gram's surgery?*
> **THEM:** *Oh gosh! Sorry, I forgot. How'd it go?*

US: *Not so well . . . You mean it never crossed your mind at all today?*

THEM: *Sorry, I had a really busy day, then Tandy just let go on me. I have a ton of homework, and Mr. Gaines was in a really bad mood, so we had to stay after to do makeup work. [And on and on . . .]*

As always, we choose our response carefully, aware that regardless of how justified our hurt or anger, anything we say diminishes under the weight of adolescent anguish.

US: *I understand that you have a lot going on, but I wish you had thought about Gram as well. Why not give her a call now so she understands that you haven't forgotten her?*

No matter how many lectures, consequences, or lessons we deliver, we cannot alter a basic fact of adolescence: Their default perspective is their own. Are they capable of taking another's perspective? Sure; just not initially or consistently. Does this mean they are callous human beings or we have spoiled them beyond repair? No, although most of our adolescents have been raised by child-centered parents. Does this leave us with no choice but to lower the consequence boom in the hope that it shakes loose their adolescent egocentrism? No doubt many of us have tried this route and discovered that any impact is short-lived, mostly because their brains are so shortsighted. Does this mean we have no recourse but to stand by and count the adolescent seconds until they discover the hidden (at least for them) treasures of adulthood, like multiple perspectives, judgment, and the ability to reflect on their decisions? Not at all.

Instead, we mix and remix the blend and balance of a host

of roles, from coach to fan, from consultant to manager. We neither waver nor withdraw our support. As long as we don't lure them using guilt. As long as we stay in touch and hold them accountable when they do make a wrong turn. There is no guidepost more visible, more important, or more durable than the one we offer.

TIME IS ON THEIR SIDE

IN THE ALTERED STATE OF ADOLESCENCE, IT'S NOT JUST THEIR mirrors that are distorted. Time, too, runs at a different clock speed. For example, many of us (often mistakenly) assume that the phrase *When I'm finished . . .* bears some relationship to time. Not so if our adolescents are busy nursing myriad critical, or at least immediate, needs, such as finishing a TV show, navigating a group chat or video conference, and planning the weekend's activities. In fact, any request, demand, or requirement not offering immediate gratification can trigger a rash reaction. Our adolescents' inability to envision outcomes or consequences (*If you just do it now, you can spare yourself from my wrath later*) only intensifies their irritation. Hence, a relatively simple request becomes a harangue; a slight admonishment is perceived as "yelling" at them; accusations boomerang.

> **THEM:** *Why are you always yelling at me? Calm down! Can't I do anything right? I'll clean up the kitchen as soon as I'm finished [whatever . . .]*

By far the most effective response to an outburst is to say nothing—at least not right away. Nothing quells or seizes control over an uprising faster or more effectively than silence. Conversely, nothing fans an adolescent fire better than a sentence beginning with *Don't you dare—!* Why? Because it begs the response every adolescent longs for: *Just watch me!*

Alternatively, we engage freely in a much more revealing internal conversation: Do we want them to clean up the kitchen *right this second* because we're irked at them for something else, or because we're sick of looking at the mess, or perhaps because they have reneged one too many times on an understood family obligation? When our reasons are clear, usually the words we choose to convey them are, too. And if our words are clear, then chances are we can avoid one of their most effective time (and mind) traps, the circular argument. Whether energized by a need to exercise their abstract reasoning function or to test their resistance mechanisms, adolescents seem to have limitless time and energy to spend on parental polemics. (Don't forget the *Last Word* or *Name That Tune* games. See chapter 3, Controlling Them Is Not the Point.)

> **US:** *I know you have other stuff you'd much rather be doing right now but cleaning the kitchen is your job, and part of doing your job is getting it done in a timely way so that the rest of us can use the kitchen without having to work around dirty dishes and counters. That's the deal we talked about; that's the deal you agreed to. If you want to change it, bring me a proposal, but not until you have held up your end.*
> **THEM:** *But, listen, just listen to me a minute.*
> **TRANSLATION:** *Don't try to interrupt me or I'll brand you as one of those parents who don't listen to their kids.*
> **THEM:** *I just need to explain something . . .*

We go as many rounds as make sense or that we can tolerate without losing our cool, then, like a policeman directing traffic, we gesture, rather than speak a thousand (authoritative) words. When enough is enough, a simple hand indicating *Stop!* says it all. To reinforce the (wordless) message, we accomplish the impossible for most of us: *We walk away.* To an adolescent, *no* words often speak louder than a raft of misspent ones. If we must, we allow ourselves a solitary time-based reference: *Later!*

To stay in touch, we may have to adjust our clocks to theirs, at least for a decade or so. They can't always tell our time; we should at least understand how to tell theirs.

THE ART OF THE ADOLESCENT CONVERSATION

WE MAY BE SURPRISED AT HOW MUCH DATA A SIMPLE BUT SPE-cific declarative sentence (*cum* question) can yield: *I heard Camilla got grounded,* or *I was thinking about your English teacher, Mr. Evans, and how he really seems to like it when students ask for extra help* . . .

Ferreting (useful) information from an adolescent requires the cunning of a detective tempered with the sensibility of an artist. While our probes are often searching for specific answers to specific questions, they are also monitoring the overall functionality and performance of the adolescent system. Or sometimes, we just like their company. Regardless of our motivations, some of us are better at the art of conversation than others. Innate abilities aside, we can all apply some basic *Dos* and *Don'ts.*

-------------------------------- **DO** --------------------------------

■ **Entertain the possibility that the conversations we think we're having are often about something else.** Next time we step on a conversational land mine and witness an inexplicable adolescent explosion, assume that there may well be something we don't know about that's bothering them. Often, we can find out by gently probing, but be prepared for a time delay.

■ **Let them spill their beans at their own pace.** Don't be surprised to find small strains from previous conversations reappearing as whole new themes in later ones.

> THEM: *Remember I was telling you about how a bunch of senior guys came for cake at Gwinny's fourteenth birthday party?*
> US: *Yes [even if we don't—or do only vaguely].*
> THEM: *Well, they weren't exactly invited, and when we went downstairs Birge had a flask.*
> US: *Really? How come you didn't mention this before?*
> THEM: *I don't know . . .*

Just because we're frequently out of step with the adolescent pace of things doesn't mean we can't keep up. Timing is everything, unless, of course, it's irrelevant.

> US: *So then what happened . . . ?*

■ **Digest first, follow up later** (as in a few hours or even days, not minutes). When in doubt . . . say nothing—or, as our adolescents would say, *chill.* Not every confession or confidence or comment begs a response, at least not immediately.

■ **Be specific, if possible using case scenarios.** If we want to know whether there was alcohol at a party, rather than interrogate—*Was there drinking?* or even *Who was drinking?* we try something like: *Was there any* *vodka [*or something else*] available to add to drinks?* Or, if sex is the target, rather than asking *Were a lot of kids hooking up?* we get even more specific, *Do kids who want to have oral sex find a place to do it privately, or do they just go off to a corner?* By probing directly at the source we're more apt to get more than a monosyllabic response.

■ **Vary questioning techniques.** Questions don't always have to be stated as interrogatories—see above. If one approach doesn't work, try another: *You won't believe what I heard today!* or *Did you know . . . ?*

■ **Remember that most adolescents view their number one job as pleasing us.** Therefore, most of their answers reveal only what they think we want to hear. To get more, ask.

■ **Be ready with a probing follow-up.** Since the tender areas don't always show, we probe carefully but opportunistically, watching their reactions, testing their tolerance. *And then what happened? Where was Frankie during all this?*

■ **Tell the truth.** Regardless of the question. They can tell if we don't. But they can't tell if we don't tell all.

■ **Know when to stop—and stop!** They'll let us know when. We just have to do it.

DON'T

■ **Don't interview for pain.** They may not be as bothered or upset about something as we think they are (or as we are). The last thing we want, or they need, is to invite trouble.

■ **Don't ask questions that come across as judgments.** Questions, for instance, like *Why do you always* *wear your hair like that?* or *Why do you have to listen to that music?* rarely yield a satisfactory answer. Maybe it's the *Why do you . . .* part that launches the accusation. Instead, try leading with reinforcement: *You know, I liked the CD you were just listening to a lot better than the one before it. Who was that?* or *Joni was telling me the other day how much she loves your hair when it's up. Me too.*

■ **Don't expect volunteers.** In many ways, adolescents are like misers, at least as far as we're concerned. They covet that which makes them feel comfortable, whether it's an old sweatshirt or a CD; they play their thoughts close to their chests; and they conserve information as if it were water in the desert. They don't readily acknowledge the sacrifices of others, or willingly offer much assistance. They are too involved in their own high-stakes game of self-discovery, which they are petrified of losing. Our adolescents keep things from us for many reasons, some innocent, some not so. Sometimes they simply want time and space to test our advice, without being reminded.

■ **Don't be afraid to tell "stories."** Stories offer a unique opportunity to show off our creativity. Also known as parental poetic license, storytelling dispenses advice much more effectively than one of our perseverant lectures. *Did I ever tell you the story of my friend Kitty who . . .* Be assured that they will *usually* listen (whether or not they let on)—and that they will apply a discount. Since every good story has a moral, we seize any opportunity to convey one.

■ **Don't stop asking questions, even if they make us feel as though we're intruding.** But . . . (see next bullet)

- **Don't pummel them with questions.** Be patient through the silences and make sure they're finished before launching the next question.
- **As always, don't ask if we're not ready to hear the answer.**

By far, our biggest creative challenge lies in outpsyching our adolescents. Not so we can celebrate our cleverness, or anoint ourselves winners and them losers, but so we can ask the right questions to keep the conversation going.

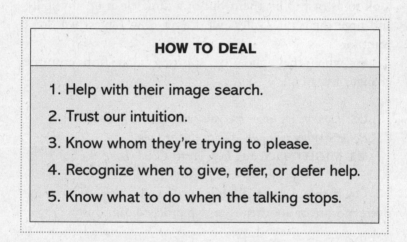

HOW TO DEAL

1. Help with their image search.

2. Trust our intuition.

3. Know whom they're trying to please.

4. Recognize when to give, refer, or defer help.

5. Know what to do when the talking stops.

1. Help with Their Image Search

Few of us have the fortitude or cunning to compete with the media juggernaut, especially with its effect on our teenagers. Those of us who have tried probably discovered a devotion far deeper than this month's fashion trend or media-anointed idol. Like the innocently expectant Barbie dolls and the ruggedly immortal GI Joes of so many childhoods, media-conjured identities offer adolescents a world in which to play

out their fantasies. No wonder they form such strong attachments to these media caricatures.

So where does that leave us? Where we've always been:
right in the center of their universes. Despite, and perhaps
even because of, the intensity of these media attachments, the
quick-to-react but slow-to-mature adolescent brain needs
even more help sorting through the debris cluttering the path
to who and what they will become. Yes, they look to peers
and teachers and coaches for guidance and direction, but
none wields the influence that we do. Most adolescents still
look to us first to lift them out of a funk, clean up any spills,
and urge them on. Unless we forget how. Unless we don't
want to.

So when they glide by sporting their fifth costume
change, instead of:

> **US:** *How many times are you going to change your*
> *clothes? What was wrong with the first one?*
> **WE MIGHT TRY:** *You look great! Good choice.*

Or, if the alarm bell tolls too loudly because of some
overexposure or another, then we proceed cautiously:

> **US:** *I know you know where our limits of respectability*
> *[show respect] lie. It makes me very uncomfortable seeing*
> *that much [bare skin, blue hair, underwear exposed].*
> **NOT:** *You may want to look like some drugged-out rock*
> *star, but that just doesn't go in this house!*

What's wrong with this response? It begs a showdown,
and few of us survive a showdown without somebody getting
hurt. Like a toothache, sometimes showdowns are unavoid-
able, but most of us prefer the preventive route.

INSTEAD: *I know it's a look for a lot of kids. But if it makes me uncomfortable, then it's going to make others uncomfortable, too. So see if you can find an alternative that works for all of us. I really like that shirt; maybe just a different [*pair of pants, shoes*].*

Desperate to avoid getting caught in another adolescent quagmire, we constantly devise detours. If all else fails, we tighten our grip on patience and confront the snarl head-on.

THEM: *Well, too bad. I'm wearing it. It's not my problem that you don't like it—it's yours!*

We can always adopt the *Love and Logic* approach:[13]

US: *I know [*show empathy*] . . . I guess we just differ on this. So what are you going to do about it?*
THEM: *Nothing! I told you already! [*Knowing that this adolescent rage, too, shall pass—we let it.*]*
US: *Want to know what other kids have done in these situations? [*Offer alternatives*].*
THEM: *No-oo! . . . Okay, what?*
US: *Well, some wear something that they know satisfies us and then change later.*
TRANSLATION: *I'm not as dumb as I look!*
US: *Or some just storm out, leaving everybody feeling angry and bad. Or they don't go at all. Those are the things I can think of. Ultimately, of course, it's up to you. And as you know, all I really care about is that you show respect—to yourself, to us and the Rules of Play, and to others. You're a great-looking kid no matter what you wear.*

In other words, we give them enough alternatives to reject, ranging from outlandish to reasonable, fastidiously avoiding the one we favor, and hope that they end up with a choice we both can live with.

And that's where we leave it. If we really can't live with their choice, then we clink rather than clang the consequence bell:

> **US:** *If you choose not to respect our Rules of Play, then I'll need to think of a consequence. Let me ponder what makes sense, and we'll discuss it later.*

Ultimately, we want the battles to be of *our* choosing, not theirs. Making them wait, and anticipate the potential consequences, is half of it. Will the outcomes always end up where we wanted? No. Have we made an impression? Yes, at least for now—and maybe longer.

Just as parenting is not a right but a conscious decision, our adolescents are not meant to embody our image and likeness; we are meant to assist in their search for their own. The best way to do that is to focus our efforts on two critical self-image enhancers: reinforcement and assessment.

Reinforcement, as opposed to criticism, helps our adolescents build a natural defense against malignant depressive feelings. And by constantly but subtly assessing their actions, nonactions, and reactions, we remain on the lookout for dramatic changes or other danger signs. While we cannot prevent the melancholy moods, or the outbursts, we can apply the kind of psycho-salve that propels their belief that, with effort, they can do the "it" that they're not sure they can. There is no such thing as too much of the right kind of reinforcement; there is never a wrong time to give it.

2. Trust Our Intuition

However distorted their mirrors, however used or abused we feel, we keep our intuition radar tuned and primed, and ourselves in a position to read it. We pursue anything (a comment, an action, an e-mail) that signals despair—even if the incident seems isolated or insignificant. Even if it's just hearsay. When safety is in question, all evidence is admissible, including seemingly idle, passing comments such as: *Life sucks. It's no use. Nothing matters. I just want to get away from all this.*

> **US:** *I've been hearing you say things like this for a couple of weeks and I'm getting worried because you sound so hopeless. Do things ever seem to get better?*

Depending on their temperaments (see chapter 3, Controlling Them Is Not the Point), most adolescents give off depressive signals or stress alarms, some louder than others. These signals, similar in initial appearance to chronic anxiety, need only be worrisome if they persist over time or seem extreme either in their tone or in their terms. If the answers to our questions fall into the *Yeah, sometimes* category, then we keep watching, subtly but vigilantly. If the answer falls into the *It's never going to get better* category, we respond more proactively:

> **US:** *You know you don't have to feel this way. We all feel bad sometimes, but no one needs to feel bad all the time. How about if I find someone for you to talk to? There are lots of people who are really good at helping kids like you feel better.*

The strongest risk factors for young people—what we need to be watching and listening for—are depression, alcohol or drug use, and aggressive or disruptive behaviors. Research also shows that more than 70 percent of people who commit suicide discuss their intentions with someone beforehand.[14] (Another reason to get to know their friends; see chapter 5, Friends Don't Matter as Much as We May Think.)

Despair can wear many disguises. It's up to us to see through them. Our gut instincts remain our best line of defense. This may be one of our most important parenting powers.

Just because we own refrigerators doesn't mean we know how to fix them, or even what makes them break down. That we've owned a lot of them or that they've lasted a long time doesn't automatically make us experts regarding their mechanics. No, adolescents are not refrigerators; nor are they things. And owning a refrigerator is not the same as raising a child. Still, just because we're doing the best parenting job we know how, and boast a great track record to prove it, doesn't mean a particular adolescent won't go wrong or, worse, break down. Even the lucky ones, or the parents who seem to breed stars, need a little help along the way. Adolescence presents enough unstable variables—from uncultivated brains, to expanding bodies, to desperate longings for so many things, including separation from us—to challenge, if not stymie, even the pros. Even though protecting, nourishing, and sheltering our kids has been our single biggest life investment, it hasn't necessarily earned us all the answers. Maybe it's okay to admit (even to our adolescents) that we aren't always right and don't always know.

While we play a critical role in shaping *how* our adolescents think about the image they see in the mirror, we can no more change that image than alter the mirror. And yet, in the background of their mirrored reflections, there we are, like wallpaper, our patterns muted but still soothing, familiar, blending into their lives, connecting the seams, defining the edges—containing.

3. Know Whom They're Trying to Please

One of the most elusive parenting struggles we face is how to motivate our adolescents. To that end, without warning or much effort, we become addicted to the merest hint of an interest on their part and dedicate ourselves to nurturing it into full-scale promise. We often overlook the profound difference between extrinsic motivation (that which they do for someone else or for external reward, such as money or pleasing us) and intrinsic motivation (that which they do for the sheer love of it). The latter motivation bounces them out of bed in the morning, makes them finish their homework on Friday night, or prompts them to voluntarily talk to us—or even to other adults: Intrinsic motivation naturally secretes dopamine leaving them thirsty to do, try, explore more).

> **US:** *C'mon! You can do better than this. We're not investing all this money in [you name it] only to watch you act like you don't even care. Money doesn't grow on trees, you know. We've come too far for you to embarrass us this way.*

> vs.

> **US:** *It sounds like you're feeling pretty exhausted. And the harder you work, the harder a goal can sometimes appear. But, in the end, the achievement will be yours and no one else's and that's what you—and we—will be most proud of.*

If our adolescent's success was a truly purchasable commodity, most of us would have invested much more than we already have in the accoutrement and the advocacy that we hope will make it so.

Some of us treat their search for success as our own, a coveted holding that we monitor carefully, setting goals, expecting only the highest rate of return, intruding as a right, strategically meting out approvals and disapprovals. High stakes and highly personal. Others of us choose to let our investment in our children mature over time, remain patient as it variously gains and loses ground, recoups from failures, surges unexpectedly. So confident are we in their worth, we continue to invest in their success, reaping our rewards from theirs, not the other way around.

Our adolescents learn the difference, quickly, innately, between success *they* create from their own raw materials, and that which they construct artificially for show. Our adolescents know, as intimately as they know self-doubt, the feelings of unearned or ill-gotten success born out of fear of disappointment, disapproval, even rejection.

Those of us who have achieved personal success did so in no small measure because we *believed* we could. Sure, we were propelled by strong influencers, persuaded by advocates, driven by expectations. But honest self-reflection will likely reveal that we achieved what we did autonomously, resisting temptation, using the most reliable and rewarding of all currencies, our own effort. Success comes in many shapes and sizes. Sometimes for others to see, sometimes not. Sometimes earning us public credit, sometimes not. When success is real, none of this matters because we know we own the source. But when success comes discounted or compromised, so do the rewards.

Our adolescents are not the only ones growing up during

their childhoods. We too are being raised as parents, educated by myriad schools of thought. Among the most convincing is that which purports that praise motivates, and the more the better. But like many life lessons, the truth is more complex. Praise without internal buy-in, belief, and proof pokes holes in the very sense of self it is trying to inflate. Like any proof, self-worth or self-efficacy cannot be conjured. It cannot be demanded or commanded. Its source is itself, waiting to be worked out, its value revealed. Self-efficacy springs internal from desire, conviction, persistence, and hard work; it self-replenishes. It is not ours to possess; many have tried and been run aground by disappointment. Mozart may have begun composing and playing the clavier before royalty as of age four, but he did not assume an official position as a musician until age seventeen. In between, he practiced.

When we attempt to motivate extrinsically, we heap praise upon promise convincing ourselves perhaps, but never our adolescents, that they are great at this or that, and that greatness will lead to great things, both for them—and us. Ever eager to please us, they pore over their books, attack their exams, set their alarms, attend extra practices, ratchet up the scores.

But what happens when progress wanes, or worse, failure strikes? When the veneer of interest in this sport or that lesson cracks under its own weight? When lack of energy drains their wills, and their egos deflate before our eyes? What happens when our *Whys?* and *What happeneds?* echo back on us, the hollow sound of our own voices?

I don't know is often the only response they can muster. And they mean it. How are they supposed to construct their real selves when they are too busy hiding inside a false one? What happens when they lack the resources and strategies to yank themselves from the clutches of failure or disappointment? When they lack the internal scaffolding to climb out of a funk? When they are afraid to admit failure?

Let's compare two approaches:

US: *What's the story with your math grade this term? You're really smart in math; this should be your best grade, not your worst!*
THEM: I know!!! *My teacher sucked. He really didn't get me. I don't know what his problem is. . . .*
US: *Well, you better talk to him and get it together. You need that A.*

vs.

US: *Your math grade really suffered this term. Any idea why?*
THEM: *I know!!! My teacher sucked. I don't know what his problem is. . . .*
US: *Being smart or good at something doesn't mean you don't have to work hard at it. Olympic athletes may have talent but they also put in thousands of hours of practice. Would you say that you put in the hours needed to do well in math this term?*

A recent survey showed that over 40 percent of thirteen- to fourteen-year-olds and nearly 60 percent of fifteen- to seventeen-year-olds feel stressed on a daily basis.[15] Incidents of diagnosed adolescent stress, and its more serious counterparts—anxiety disorders and depression—are up to eight times higher than in our own adolescence.[16] Adolescent stress eats away at the essential building blocks of their psychological protein, leaving them weak and depleted.[17] (See Stress and the Adolescent Brain, under Their Brains Are to Blame.)

The blame labels for the increase in adolescent stress levels vary from school pressures to performance pressures to familial and societal pressures to be perfect. So, if the lever is pressure, who holds the best position to raise and lower it? Not our adolescents. They are way too busy inhaling its vapors. Teachers? Sure, in as much as they enable, or even label, our children's success, or lack thereof. But no hand has a firmer grasp on the pressure levers than ours. We adjust the levers with the best of intentions: to keep them afloat, to buoy their confidence. Look, they got chosen, didn't they? Appear happy, don't they? And so we buoy. Who else, if not us?

If they seem exhausted, not talking much anymore, distracted, withdrawn, we encourage them, and ourselves: *They're just tired. They're young, resilient. They'll make up for it over vacation. . . .*

Although we're all born with potential, it can be fed from without, but must be nurtured from within to achieve full growth. Like learning, potential accumulates in chunks, builds on itself, gets reinforced through experience, one success—and failure—at a time: a math concept untangled (despite a trail of wrong answers), a hit in a game (despite a slew of strikeouts), one perfect measure of a song (despite a headache-inducing score of flat notes). Step-by-step, small goal by small goal, we encourage both the wins and the losses for what they teach our adolescents—our eyes not on the lofty endgame, but the small victories that lead there. According to a recent survey, only 42 percent of ten- to eighteen-year-olds say they are energetically pursuing their own goals and only 35 percent know how to find ways around the obstacles impeding them.[18] If not their own goals, then whose are they pursuing? An achiever is someone who can identify a goal, a strategy to address it, and the willingness to work to accomplish it. Achievers know how to make both the wins and losses count.

Just as we share features, characteristics, and even body types with our adolescents, we also share a link to their psychology, which perhaps explains a recent study linking parental control and child anxiety. Anxious parents make for anxious kids.[19]

Well prior to adolescence, our children learn how to please. But *whom* they should be pleasing, and *why*, are much harder concepts to grasp because they must first *know* themselves in order to be able to *please* themselves.

The differences are subtle, but never lost on an adolescent.

4. Recognize When to Give, Refer, or Defer Help

As with many illnesses, much more is known about the symptoms of depression than the causes. We do know that depression can run in families and be triggered by an acute physical illness or another traumatic life event, such as death, loss of a loved one, divorce, or even a move. Low self-esteem, a demon dwelling on many an adolescent doorstep, also increases vulnerability to depression. While *vulnerability* is an adolescent watchword, *depression* is not. And so we guard against this melancholy intruder by helping expose its many disguises. Because no one else will ever be as vigilant or concerned, we search for the sometimes subtle inconsistencies or incongruities lurking amid already chaotic adolescent behavior, like the two-headed squirrel blending into the muted tree bark in the *What's Wrong with This Picture* game.

Below is a partial checklist of depressive symptoms that, in combination or persistent over time (two or more for a period of longer than two weeks), could signal a clinical depression that warrants professional treatment.

- Are they eating significantly more or less?
- Are they sleeping significantly more or less?
- Do they show significant weight gain or loss without appearing to alter their diets?
- Did they suddenly drop out or lose interest in previous involvements or activities?
- Do they seem persistently irritable, listless, or depressed— sad, empty, tearful?
- Do they suddenly seem to have difficulty concentrating, making decisions, or mustering energy to participate?
- Do they seem to feel exceedingly guilty, worthless, or helpless?
- Are they commenting about hurting themselves or others, or death or suicide (*You won't be seeing me around; I won't be a problem much longer*)?
- Do they complain of chronic aches or pains that don't respond to treatment?

Just because we know the location of our adolescents' birthmarks and the sound of their laughter better than anyone else doesn't mean we are either the cause or the cure for all that ails them. While we, hopefully, remain their most sought-after model and adviser, our adolescents' most effective teacher is now their own experience, including—perhaps most important—their own mistakes.

Just as we wielded the power to stunt their early physical development, we now wield the power to disable a primary mechanism of self-discovery—failure. Part of keeping our adolescents safe is knowing when to nourish and shelter them, and when to let them go it alone, even if it means leaving them standing in the cold. Maybe they need to demonstrate that they, too, are strong enough to brave the elements and survive, just as we were. Sometimes the best shelter we can provide is none at all.

5 Know What to Do When the Talking Stops

If we are worried about their inability to bounce back from common adolescent defeats, and they don't respond to our usual home remedies, then a teenager may be in need of professional intervention by trained practitioners. In the meantime, we can still try myriad parental antidotes to ease any discomfort. These include:

- **Listen with special interest and attention to detail.** A willing ear may be all the solace they're seeking. And we may need, at some point, to recount this information to a professional.
- **Convey concern.** *I'm worried because you have been sounding so down lately. You must really be feeling overwhelmed by everything.*
- **Ask direct questions.** Even if it means prying the answers from their mouths, regardless of concern about opening the suggestion kimono. Even if it means taking another tongue-lashing.

   US: *Have you been feeling depressed? Are you thinking about hurting yourself or ending your life? I need to know more about what you mean by that comment . . .*
   THEM: *Are you crazy? What are you talking about?!*

   What is one more ridicule-inflicted bruise? It won't be our first—or our last. It can't hurt as much as guilt or blame. It can't wrench as much as grief or loss.

■ **Respect their privacy but don't let it hold us hostage.** There is a difference between secrecy and privacy, just as there is a difference between nosiness and concern. We can't afford to let privacy be a cloak for danger or potential danger. We can't reach what we can't see; we won't recognize what we don't know about; we won't find out without curiosity. While respecting adolescents' privacy is critical to establishing and maintaining mutual trust and respect, our primary job remains to keep them safe. To do that, we need information. By ignoring or neglecting information, we may be letting them down, not protecting them.

The face in the adolescent mirror reflects a full range of emotions, from love to loathing, admiration to rejection. Voyeurs with a cause, we linger near enough to keep watch, careful not to intrude unless necessary. While our teenagers may not always want our presence, we want them to sense it.

As they launch on countless excursions to the borders of adulthood, we ask only that they stay safe, show respect, and stay in touch. Each time they return, we reinforce and assess, all while scanning for reassurance that all is well—or not.

FRIENDS DON'T MATTER AS MUCH AS WE MAY THINK

OFTEN, WE OBSERVE OUR ADOLESCENTS AS IF STRANDED IN another orbit, unable to compete with the gravitational pull toward their peer planets. We struggle to keep our adolescents in our line of sight as they career from moment to moment, buffeted by constantly changing conditions. Exhilarated by their own flashes of brilliance and stimulated by an expanding brain, they seek safety in numbers and affirmation in kinship.

We content ourselves with the role of savvy bystander, trying to understand and evaluate the appeal—and influence—of these new objects of their desire or affection. No longer the consistent focal point of their universe, we treasure the moments when our paths coincide, a car ride here, a family meal there.

FRIENDS VERSUS COMPANIONS

IN ADOLESCENCE, FRIENDSHIPS TAKE ON NEW DIMENSIONS AND meanings that play out in an exclusive interactive theater

complete with roles and scripts and scenes waiting to be performed. On this stage, all cast members count as "friends," and
improvisation is a rite of passage. Once the primary contrib-
utor to their scripts, we now only hope for an editing credit.
How did the stars of these one-person adolescent shows become so consumed with their own fame?

Recent studies on use of media by the eight- to-eighteen-
year-old set reinforce what we have all observed: a dramatic
increase in hours spent in front of some kind of screen, especially cell phones and computers; 93 percent now go online
and spend an average of 53 hours per week, or 7.38 hours per
day. Accounting for the voracious multitasking appetites of
these users, their daily media diet actually comes closer to 11
hours.[1]

How they are consuming this media is also changing
rapidly. Cell phones, iPods, and MP3 players are overtaking
the standard television set with cell phone ownership jump-
ing from 39 to 75 percent[2] and iPods and MP3 players from
18 to 76 percent over the past five years.[3]

Adolescents spend more time *watching* media on their cell
phones than they do talking on them (and this doesn't include
texting). Yet, 45 percent report the television always on at
home, regardless of whether someone is watching, and two
thirds report its steady din as a backdrop to meals.[4] While
tweeting is slower to gain ground with early-to-mid adolescents, Facebook has become as much about photo-sharing as
it is about soul-baring.

And where are we amid all this media bingeing? If only 5
percent of adolescents between eight and eighteen report that
their parents watch TV along with them, what percent of us
are joining them to listen to music, play video games
(although there is evidence that gamer parents do game with
their kids), or use the computer, let alone know what their

adolescent's Facebook pages look like? Rather than allow them to use these incredible shrinking personal screens to force us out of their lives, we need to find a way to make co-viewing, or somehow sharing, if not a condition, than an acceptable part of their online lives. For instance, when we make those spontaneous visits to their rooms (See chapter 3, Games It's Okay to Play, under Controlling Them Is Not the Point), lie down on their beds while they're online, or pull up a chair (*saying nothing!*). Co-view—and learn. Or, when in midconversation with us, their fingers let loose on cell phone keypads like a piano virtuoso, join in. Send your own text to them!

> **THEM:** *Mom, what are you doing?*
> **US:** *What do you mean?*
> **THEM:** Why *are you texting me? I'm right here!*
> **US:** *I know. I thought we were having a conversation, and suddenly you were texting someone else. So, I thought I'd join the fun. . . .*
> **THEM:** *You're ridiculous!*
> **US:** *It is kind of ridiculous, isn't it, that text interruptions are okay. But if a person barged in on our conversation, it would seem rude.*
> **THEM:** *Okay, I'm done, so what were you saying?*
> **US:** *So what was that flurry all about? Everything okay?*
> *[*Keep it quick, light, and to the point. They might even share a morsel or two.*]*

Is this tidal wave of available media so overwhelming that only three in ten of us impose rules about time spent using said media?[5] Despite proof that media usage *does* decline when limits are set—and grades *are* shown to improve with lighter use? Despite personal anecdotes about grade slippage among heavy media users, borne out by bona fide studies? Is their ambidexterity or cleverness so accomplished that we really don't notice them texting through meals and beneath the bedcovers? Or do we just look the other way to avoid another confrontation?

> **THEM:** *What's that?*
> **US:** *It's a new basket I bought. It's for storing our cell phones while we're having dinner. [*Or doing anything "family."*] That will make it easier to abide by the family rule. I thought we could use it during homework time as well! [*Remember, by far the hardest part of establishing rules is enforcing them—consistently, reliably and predictably.]*

We set the rules and categorize them as part of Showing Respect. That way, if they choose not to play, we've already explained the consequences.

Perhaps because we willingly accept irony as a fact of life, we continue to pressure, expect, hover, and spend countless dollars trying to ensure their unique brand of stardom while feeding a growing dependency on media substances proven to be rewiring their brains, affecting their sleep and school performance, and establishing norms regarding everything from sex to plagiarism to decision making.

Despite proven correlations between deep reading and vocabulary accumulation, and ultimately SAT scores, time spent reading from traditional sources such as books, newspapers, and magazines continues to decline. If asked, most adolescents will easily recall a favorite childhood book, even where they were when they read it. Ask them whether their parents are readers, and find no hesitation in their response. No need to ask whether an adolescent reads deeply, just listen to him speak, or read her writing. We not only are what we read, but how we read it.

More than a friend, media has become a ubiquitous superpeer whose presence in our homes threatens to replace the hearth. When was the last time we sat down with our adolescents to watch or play or even converse? Is it any wonder that they stop inviting us to join in? When was the last time they did and we politely declined, citing a laundry list of obligations, not to mention our own disinterest?

As if by default, most adolescents choose gadgetry as their preferred downtime activity. For many, it offers the security of a constant and nonjudgmental companion. This electronic accompaniment has become so ingrained in our lives, we may have underestimated the trade-offs between company and actual human interaction. In our struggle to plug the slow but steady leakage of time with our kids, have we unwittingly created a false sense of togetherness?

> **US:** *You didn't answer my question. [Smile a little so your voice does, too.]*
> **THEM:** *Oh sorry, I was just finishing something . . .*
> **US:** *What? Like Facebook something or homework something?*
> **THEM:** *Chill, I'm here, aren't I?*
> **US:** *Not really . . .*
> **THEM:** *Well, you're checking your e-mail or texting just as much, you know. It's not just me . . .*

Social Friendworking

EVEN "HANGING OUT" WITH FRIENDS, THE SACRED RIGHT OF adolescence and an essential element of identity formation and social norming, has undergone its own version of a mash-up—mingling in-the-flesh interactions with parallel online play, text-ersations, and snooping at nth degrees of separation. A recent Pew Study found that over half of the 75 percent of teens thirteen to seventeen who use cell phones send fifty text messages a day (that's 1,500 per month) and one third send over one hundred text messages a day (that's more than 3,000 per month). By comparison, phone calls average 140 per month, and many of those are to parents as a way of keeping in touch.[6]

Cell phones are to adolescents what their love objects were to them as toddlers and their vbfs (very best friends) were to them as grade schoolers. Less cuddly, but just as attached, these sleeker, slicker replacements remain the go-betweens for a still daunting outside world. An all-in-one communication device, cell phones record, plan, manage, and process their personal dominions. As the capabilities of these mechanical manna expand, so does our adolescents' dependency. And we easily justify their intrusive existence because (a) they keep *us* in touch with *our adolescents,* and (b) many of us are just as enamored and addicted as they are.

Happy to forgo the awkwardness of the initial overture, or the intimidation of a hallway or school bus rebuff, our adolescents lay miles of social groundwork getting to know the likes, dislikes, friends, and nonfriends of potential friends from afar, before the first invitation is ever sent. The once highly exclusive "popular" circles become both more permeable and more visible as friends of friends enter the carefully crafted, made-for-public-viewing version of each other's worlds. While no one likes to sit alone in the cafeteria, such popularity blemishes can be masked or even mitigated by an impressive friend count or an active Wall. Social friendworking offers adolescents a sneak peek, if not a passport, into fiefdoms heretofore impenetrable.

Navigating social forays from the safety of one's own cockpit allows an adolescent to adventure more freely, post more wildly, and try on more personas, while eliminating such time-wasting hassles as soliciting rides, securing a car, walking, or spending time, energy, or money just to parallel play on their computers. Even the teenage driving right of passage appears to have ceded to a more virtual one. New findings link a significant decrease in U.S. auto sales, in part, to a decline in car usage by teenagers who are prefering to socialize from the comfort of their own computers.[7]

In these worlds, snippets of identities and egos get texted, posted, and punctured. Flirtations either reach their intended targets or just float featherlike through the ethernet with no particular destination or accountability. Friends get confirmed with less likelihood of becoming real than a personal ad. And darts get thrown with impunity, despite potentially devastating impact.

Of the 146 million (and growing rapidly) U.S.-based users of Facebook, 37 percent are over thirty-five (compared to 9 percent of thirteen- to seventeen-year-olds), and 31 percent of eighteen- to twenty-four-year-olds. The over fifty-five set of users increased almost 60 percent to nearly 11 percent of that demographic in one year.[8] If teachers, employers, colleges, and even grandparents can wend their way to our adolescents' sites, then privacy doesn't really hold as a

reason for excluding us. And if a first parenting try at friend-
ing doesn't succeed, try, try again (see chapter 1, Technology
and the Adolescent Brain, under Their Brains Are to Blame).

> **US:** *I know you've said in the past that you don't want to
> friend me, but can you explain once more what you're
> worried about?*
>
> **THEM:** *You're kidding, right? It's MY place to be with
> MY friends. It would be like you hanging out in my room
> when I have friends over.*
>
> **US:** *I understand that concern, and I respect, and don't
> want to invade, your privacy, but I guess I don't understand
> what you're worried about. I don't want to control your
> Facebook site just as I wouldn't want you to control mine.
> Are there things on your site that you're afraid for me to
> see?*
>
> **THEM:** *No-oah! It would just feel like you'd be
> eavesdropping, or something.*
>
> **US:** *There's a difference between privacy and control. For
> instance, you know that lots of people: other adults, school
> officials, potential employers, college admissions people have
> ways of seeing your site—even with the privacy settings,
> right?*
>
> **THEM:** *Yeah, I've heard those stories, but that would never
> happen to me. Anyway, I'm careful. You can trust me—and
> you don't have a right to snoop!*
>
> *[*Knowing that our job is to post the warning signs
> in the hope they see them, we move on.*]*
>
> **US:** *You're right, I don't. Which is why I'm asking you.
> Just like you, to me, it's a matter of trust. Just like I
> trust that you get that you have no idea who might have
> access to something on your Wall, I hope you would*

trust me to not abuse the privilege of being friended by you.

THEM: *So why do you want to so badly? You wouldn't go snooping around in a diary of mine, would you?*

US: *Actually, it's not like a diary because people you don't even know can look at your Wall. Anyway, I see it as another way to keep in touch. And, by the way, I know how many kids have alternate sites under different names, but that's not the point, is it?*

[Sometimes just letting them know what you know is enough to convert fear of our harsh judgments into concern for their safety.]

THEM: *You just don't get it.*

US: *So, how about we try it? And if, after a month, you aren't comfortable, we can talk about it. To me, your site is like your room in this house. I will respect it, but you have to live up to the rules of play regarding what you do there. Okay?*

Wait a day or so, and issue the Facebook invitation. Wait a few more days for a confirmation. If it doesn't come, try again. All the data confirm that teen pregnancy and drug use decrease under our influence. This is just another street corner that we need to monitor, another risk we need to talk about—not ban or spy on or control. There is a big difference between a Facebook Wall as a virtual playground and a Facebook Wall as a virtual dartboard for the plethora of "just kidding" brand of adolescent insults. For parents, there is an even bigger difference between being a friend and being a friendly presence.

Even dating has redefined itself to fit the social mores of their online worlds. Access 24/7 suggests new types of intimacy that begin with a wake-up text. This parlays to an en-route-to-school text (too often from behind a wheel), which converts to face-time at school, then to an after-school homework or videogame session. An actual phone call in the evening may prove useful in speccing out a weekend plan, and a good-night text/kiss partitions a few hours of sleep and the next cycle. Indeed, textual intercourse has become a language unto itself. Just ask any practiced adolescent to interpret the true meaning of an immediate response versus a ten-minute delay after a girl texts a question to a boy, or vice versa. Or, the difference between a "yeah, maybe" and a "we'll see." Ask. It's surprising how much they'll share.

These media-based companions form a common bond, an automatic entry point into the ongoing conversation with their peers. Most of which we know nothing about. All the more reason to keep the conversation with us running on a parallel channel.

Is a Friend of Our Adolescents a Friend of Ours?

IN SEARCH OF THEIR TRUE IDENTITIES, ADOLESCENTS DEFINE, and redefine, themselves in the likeness of evolving, transient images. Friendship bonds form and dissolve at warp speed (especially in early adolescence), often dictated by an oligarchy of the *popular kids* (or a strong repulsion to them), and defined by a set of parentproof guidelines. The membership requirements range for these alliances from emulation to proof of prowess to numbers of Facebook friends or friend requests. As if on a mission to find their place in the peer universe, adolescents coalesce around a dominant electromagnetic force: the realization that parental Oz is not, after all, omniscient. Once the sole source of their attraction, our magnetism seems all but lost, replaced by, if not stronger then certainly more alluring, friends who look and act and feel like they do—or want to.

The discovery of adult fallibility in adolescence unleashes a rash of behaviors untested and untamed. While our teens are still dependent on us as their primary source of sustenance, suddenly our patterns, habits, even our lifestyles feel unexciting and uninviting. Sometimes they look at us with boredom or even disdain, as if we were a house in desperate need of redecorating. On the other hand, friends' houses, clothes, even parents, beckon. Adolescents' insatiable urge for the new makes us less worried about them talking to strangers than the fact that they have become strangers themselves. Meanwhile, we monitor the steady news feed of other parents' true stories, certain that the very next senseless act of mindlessness is coming from a peer near us, or worse, our own. Who knows what evil lurks in the shadows of our adolescents and their friends?

THE SEVEN MYTHS OF PEER INFLUENCE

BUSY TENDING THE GNAWING ITCH OF PEELING LAYERS OF INnocence, our adolescents eagerly circumvent any unnecessary encumbrances. As a result, we often find ourselves on opposite sides of the great divide between youth and adulthood. By readjusting our sights from this new perspective, we achieve a better view of the more positive, esteem-enhancing roles that peers play in our adolescents' search for themselves. In doing so, we dispel some of the insidious myths that mar the reputation of peerdom:

Myth 1. Peer Pressure in Adolescence Is Invariable

Peer influence evolves along with adolescents themselves. Younger adolescents (middle schoolers) rely on peers to establish social norms and conformity particularly regarding outward tastes in clothes, music, food, fads, and the like. Thus younger adolescents are much more susceptible to the tyranny of the popular. For girls, this equals looks, coolness, exclusivity or quantity of tags in Facebook picture albums; for boys, size and athleticism. Friendships are more about power plays than lasting relationships. Unable to think wholly for themselves, younger adolescents pledge their loyalty to the ones willing to take the lead or even a stand. That person becomes the all-powerful, albeit ephemeral, leader.

By tenth or eleventh grade, peer relationships evolve into much more complex ecosystems, similar to our own friendships. By this time, most adolescents are secure enough with their own identities that they don't need to rely so heavily on the affirmation of others. As a result, friendships are based on internal resources such as self-confidence, social competence, and independence.

Myth 2. Peer Pressure Is the Primary Reason Adolescents Get into Trouble with Sex, Drugs, and Alcohol

A recent study found that whereas peers play a significant role in spurring adolescents to engage in risky behaviors (as do stress, boredom, and curiosity), parents, along with close friends and family members, remain the biggest deterrents.[9]

Despite these findings, adolescents are actually more able to say *no* than we were.[10] This is one of the few areas where the media have provided positive role models. In fact, one study actually found that 60 percent of adolescents claimed that TV actually models how to say *no* in an undesirable sexual situation.[11] A different study found a dramatic increase in the number of kids who both see and internalize antidrug ads delivered via the media. This heightened attention and understanding has led to 42 percent claiming they are less likely to try drugs as a result.[12] This same study cites a major increase in parents as an important source for information about drug use, a key finding since those who learn about drug risks at home are 50 percent less likely to take them.[13]

While an increased sense of power (or knowledge) adds strength and dimension to the adolescent voice, too much doesn't so much corrupt as enable risk taking. This may explain the increased misuse of "friendly" prescription drugs, such as Ritalin and Adderall, readily entrusted to many adolescents to take, not take, or sell at will.

Much of the breakdown of adolescent inhibition barriers can be loosely blamed on overexposure to themes and content once considered adult and easily harvested from that unmonitored, boundless exploratorium called the Internet. Many of us have been shocked to discover graphic, sometimes grotesque, verbal free-for-alls in the guise of social networking. Few of us are clear on the best way to respond. With new psychological concerns about Facebook depression, do we intrude, forbid, rage, in an effort to control their play? For how long do we think we can prevail? Or, do we once again use these peeks into their interior lives as the basis for one more conversation about boundaries and reasonableness and judgment. About how to stay safe and show respect . . .

> **US:** *Do you know any kids who have been made fun of on Facebook?*
> **THEM:** *Not really . . . it's not a big deal.*
> **US:** *Uncle Jack told me that some kids wrote on Jesse's Wall that he's gay. He was pretty upset. Did you know about that?*
> *[*Note: When making a point, try to provide a

specific example. When possible, end with a
question.]

THEM: *Kind of . . . It was stupid.*

US: *It wasn't for Jesse, I don't think. When something like
that happens, do kids respond to defend each other, or just
let it go by?*

THEM: *It depends . . . sometimes, I guess.*

US: *I always wonder what would happen with bullying
situations if enough kids stood up to the bully, instead of
just watching. Do you?*

THEM: *It usually just goes away on its own.*

US: *Does it . . . really? Or, do kids just hope it will?*

Regardless of our reactions, adolescents of both genders
are more open and honest with each other. In particular, girls
not only feel more empowered to initiate sex, including oral
sex, they have learned to both seek and receive the kinds of
gratification they want as well.

These behaviors signal a heightened understanding of
and respect for each other's wishes, although not their vulnerability to hurt or disappointment. Unfortunately, girls remain
highly prone to the need to please, which often translates into
sex. Regardless, an empowered voice remains the single best
defense against unwanted or unhealthy peer pressure or teas-
ing; something to keep in mind in the course of our conversations with our teens.

Myth 3. Friends' Voices Overpower Our Voices

No question that the ring of a friend's voice overpowers the
clarion call of a parental warning. And there is no doubt that
two or more adolescent voices are louder and more influen-
tial than one. This is largely because friends are willing to listen for much longer and with much more interest than we

are. Not only that, they get it! Those at risk (depressed, low self-esteem, angry) will seek others with similar feelings as a way of filling an emotional gap. If adrift from us, teenagers will look elsewhere for a port in the storm. If the connections with us are in place, though, we—not they—will remain their anchors. For example, while the majority of adolescents tend to rely on peers for *information* about sex health and dating,[14] we have greater influence on their actual decision to have sex.[15] Our opinions matter.

Myth 4. Adolescents Always Prefer Spending Time with Peers Rather than Us

The sad truth is that not many families suffer from too much togetherness. On the contrary. More adolescents have had to learn to fend for themselves (perpetuating reliance on friends, TV, the Internet, and so on) and actually welcome time with family. The real question is: How often do we actually make it? Though they prefer to be with their friends, if asked, they will generally make time and space for us. The more we let them help define the shared time and space, the more we're likely to be part of it. In the interest of balance, maybe we make deals: One time they pick the meal, movie, game; the next time we get to.

Myth 5. We Were Just as Tempted by Sex, Drugs, and Alcohol as They Are

Those who purport this philosophy might do a quick comparison:

■ Was 9/11 a fact of our adolescent lives?
■ Did we have to contend with the Internet?

■ Is sexual innuendo on prime-time TV as common-place as laugh tracks were in our day?

■ How many of us had access to the kinds of indulgences our adolescents do in terms of money and material possessions?

■ Did one out of five adolescents have intercourse before their fifteenth birthday?

■ Did 55 percent of adolescents between the ages of fifteen and nineteen have oral sex?[16]

■ Did fifteen- to seventeen-year-olds have to worry about AIDS? (Interestingly, more than one quarter of today's teens don't believe that they can contract it from unprotected sex.)[17]

And the list could go on. One prominent psychologist speculates that today's adolescent is more adrift and at risk for several syndromes and in much greater degrees than we ever were. These syndromes include self-centeredness, depression, anxiety, and anger.[18] As stated throughout this book, the reasons for these heightened risks include exposure, diminished responsibilities, access to a host of temptations, technology (cell phones and the Internet, to name just two), media influence, fewer dual-parent families, and, last but not least, less parental involvement. Contrary to what we might think, the threats we faced shrivel in comparison to the risks our adolescents deal with on a daily basis. Rather than wonder why they are taking more risks at younger ages, shouldn't we be wondering what kind of adults we are enabling them to become?

Myth 6. There Is No Way to Fight the Tide of Peer Pressure

We shouldn't need to. Peers provide an essential benchmark against which our adolescents measure and define themselves.

A negative relationship with us can often transfer to negative peer relationships. Contrary to what most of us think, vulnerability to peer pressure is more internal than it is external.

Friends may be the catalysts but they are not the cause of most adolescent difficulties. Temptation abounds, as do the models for both accepting and rejecting it. While peers may provide accompaniment, they need not be accomplices. Like us, peers offer our adolescents a unique holding environment. We, as well as our adolescents' peers, offer the vital lifeblood of security and acceptance. Alone, neither we nor they offer enough.

Myth 7. Peer Influence Is More Negative than Positive

By the time adolescents begin to think abstractly (weighing choices, associating actions with consequences), the girders supporting their moral and ethical reasoning are largely in place. Peer pressure isn't really a matter of negative or positive; it is how teenagers learn to define who they are, to hear themselves think, to defend themselves. Listen closely to their conversations; rarely do we hear our teenagers trying to convince each other to do bad things. On the contrary, more often peers act as sounding boards for one another's notions of right and wrong.

Friendship Formations

AS IF CAPTIVE IN A SITUATIONAL PRESENT WITH NO VIEW OF the future, adolescents play out scene after unscripted scene with their peers as if energized by the sheer drama of it all. Protagonists and antagonists exchange roles with alarming frequency. Hearts are broken and repaired, disputes waged and resolved, all largely unbeknownst to us.

We watch from the wings, straining to discern the difference between a call for attention (*Hey, watch me!*) and a true call for assistance. While both are important to acknowledge, the former requires no action other than a nod of encouragement. The latter call is trickier to interpret because of its often scrambled signals. As long as we remain on the lookout, ready to point out and help repair a damaged Rule of Play, our adolescents usually won't stray too far.

US: *Sure, you can bring a friend to the game. Who were you thinking about?*
THEM: *I don't know. Who should I ask?*
US: *How about Kevin?*
THEM: *He can't. He's going away.*
US: *How about Casey or Schmitty?*
THEM: *They're all going to Keith's house.*
US: *Why, what's going on? Is he having a party?*
THEM: *I guess so. I don't know! I wasn't invited. Look, it's no big deal. I don't even care.*
US: *You mean, after all the times he's been here, he didn't even invite you? Well, that's the last time . . .*
THEM: *Just relax! I said it was no big deal.*

Although clearly a call for our help, the real question was *Who should I invite?* not *How can we retaliate against or even call attention to this friend who has let me down?* Let's try again.

THEM: *I don't know. Who should I ask?*
US: *How about Kevin?*
THEM: *He can't. He's going away.*
US: *How about Casey or Schmitty?*
THEM: *They're all going to Keith's house.*
US: *Okay [*leaving the handwriting on the wall

alone], who else comes to mind? Maybe someone from
outside school? I saw Anton's mother the other day. She
said he was asking about you . . .

And that may be all the push our teenagers need to go willingly back into the ring for another round. And we let them, careful not to call attention to any evident bruises. Sometimes we forget that even the ugliest bruises look worse than they feel, unless someone presses on them. Let that someone not be us.

In adolescence, the progression of friendships follows a discernible, if not predictable, path. Early on, our adolescents seem to latch on to the scent of the popular, pursuing it with rabid determination. Along the way, they learn to recognize the signs and characteristics of true friends. They discover whom they can rely on and who will abandon them when the going gets tough. They even learn how to regain their balance after tripping over an unanticipated rejection or disappointment.

Gradually (beginning about tenth grade), they begin to notice that there are many paths to friendships; some even branch off from others. Able to distinguish between their own likes and dislikes, they become more discriminating in their search criteria and more content with fewer matches. They realize that popularity is merely someone else's (usually) brand and they forge new bonds based on who they are rather than who they're not, or who they wish they were.

Never entirely free from disappointments (who is?), over time our adolescents develop the necessary skills to find their way through the elaborate and complex friendship maze. Few seem to avoid a dead-ended friendship or a misguided one. Stuck on the outside of yet another internal struggle, we try to imagine the friendship perils within.

Having trouble figuring out the lay of the friendship land

or whether an adolescent is stuck on the outskirts? Grab a piece of paper and pencil and ask them to sketch the social hierarchy of their class or group. If need be, draw a couple of circles to get them started. Ask: *Who would you put at the top? To what other group(s) would that group connect? How would you label the jocks, nerds, popular? Where would you put yourself? Do you ever cross over to another group? Where (else) would you like to be?* Adolescents coagulate; that we know. But do we know how and with whom? Many adolescents are more willing than we think to share their social ecologies. Those who aren't will merely chalk our request up to another slip of the parental tongue.

While friends may seem to command the bulk of our adolescents' attention, that does not mean they don't count on our presence. Despite a multitude of competing attractions, we stay in sight, consistent, predictable, and stable. At times, they may avoid or ignore or even take advantage of us. We (must) remain unfazed. These are merely surface wounds. We have survived much deeper ones.

HOW TO DEAL

1. Don't try to compete with their friends.

2. Commentate but don't pass judgment.

3. Get to know their friends and, if possible, their friends' parents.

4. Know what we need to know.

5. In the connection-separation tug-of-war— yield first.

1. Don't Try to Compete with Their Friends

Whatever our relationship with our adolescents, friends we are not—unless we really want to confuse them. How better to know whether our teachings have been internalized than to see them challenged? How else can we be sure of the strength of our adolescents' values unless we observe them withstanding the pressure and pull of peers? How can we know how our words have been interpreted unless we hear the translation in their context? This is not the role of a friend; it is the role of a parent.

The only reason to compete with our kids' friends is if we are in need of friends ourselves. And that is not a good enough reason to sabotage their developmental journey. Just as we can't compete with our adolescents' friends, we can't choose them, either—much to our consternation. Sometimes their choices fit easily into preconceptions. Other times, their choices are at such odds with our expectations, we resent the disruption.

> **THEM:** *Guess what? Gavin has invited me to go skiing with him this weekend. Can I go? We've been talking about it for a while, and his mom said this weekend would work. I'm so psyched!*

Even if so inclined, we suppress the urge to press the automatic *no* button and probe to understand all the implications of the request.

> **US:** *I didn't realize you had been discussing going away with Gavin. Have you two become more than friends?*
> **THEM:** *What are you talking about? No! Of course not.*

*You know that Gavin is one of my best friends. I tell him
everything. He knows as much about me as any of my
girlfriends. Plus he's a great skier. You think that just
because we want to ski together we're suddenly going out?
That's so typical!*

Recognizing such zingers for what they are—a mounting
defense in the guise of a good offense—we dodge them.

US: *Well, I'm not saying no, but I need to understand
more of the details.*
THEM: *Like what? Don't tell me that just because he's a
boy, you're going to get all uptight about this. If it were a
girlfriend, you wouldn't even hesitate.*
US: *Actually, I would. I would be asking the same
questions. I think it's great that you have a friend like
Gavin. I never did at your age, and I can see how much
fun it is. But this is also a little new for me. And it doesn't
change what I need to know to feel comfortable, like: that
you have thought through the Rules of Play, and that I
have enough information to anticipate and discuss any
concerns. Why don't you ask Gavin to have one of his
parents call me? Then we'll talk about it and decide.*

Enough said for now. If they remain stuck on the *I'm determined to get to yes here and now* tune (which can easily happen), keep changing the channels until a new refrain captures
their attention.

For many of us, the loudest interference is probably coming from the *I tell him everything . . . he knows everything about
me* comment. What does that *mean,* we wonder? Can she
really be talking to some twelve- to sixteen-year-old *boy*
about periods and crushes and hooking up and feeling fat and

that kind of everything? Could he really be talking to some twelve- to sixteen-year-old *girl* about masturbating and wet dreams and fantasies and fear of looking stupid every time he opens his mouth? *We* could never have done that; nor could anyone in our cohort. Going away for a weekend with the opposite gender only meant—or could lead to—one thing: sex (or so we were led to believe). Also called hormones, anyone who doubts their power is deluded.

Undeniably, hormones affect adolescent behavior; however, adolescent psychologist after adolescent psychologist has remarked on the positive effects of the changing, and deepening, nature of opposite-gender friendships.

For a host of reasons, ranging from media influence to tacitly condoned overexposure to each other's bodies, emotions, and primal urges, adolescents leave little to guesswork when it comes to knowledge of the opposite sex. With the kimono of societal expectations (real and imagined) yanked open, many of the elements of mystery and surprise surrounding opposite-gender relationships have been replaced by a much more open and honest communication-driven intimacy. We pine for the lost kingdom of courtship and discovery, fearing that its absence will somehow mar future relationships with a scar of regret. But our teenagers can't long for what they don't know.

If we zero in on the conversations between our adolescents' same- and opposite-gender friends, we discover that the staccato, often cryptic, conversations between boys that usually occur on the exhale of some other, usually sports- or music-related, activity take on a very different quality with girls. Nowadays, boys are forced to focus and actively listen in order to be taken seriously—so they do. Boy-to-girl-friend conversations often continue discussions begun in many personal-development-type classes, where topics range from

how many different slang terms there are for the female gen-
italia, or how to contract (or prevent contracting) a specific
type of STD. Encouraged by a plethora of appropriate and inappropriate models, adolescent boys and girls learn how to
discuss such complex (for us, taboo) issues as pregnancy, rape,
oral sex, harassment, and more.

Meanwhile, the barriers to entry to the adolescent dating
game increase in complexity. Boys resist, reluctant to subject
themselves to peer scrutiny and joshing about relinquished
control coupled with a healthy dose of fear of missing out
(aka FOMO) on coveted male camaraderie. Girls, more aware
of and willing to assert their need for parity, face a largely
conflicted, thus less inclined, pool of dating options. This conundrum has resolved into more expeditious party-packs
consisting of mixed genders and actual couples who wander
in and out during an evening's revelry. Ironically, the intrinsic
need to feel loved and cherished by a committed partner en-
dures.

Some of the most blatant examples of this raw honesty
are embedded in the social friendworking conduits, which
have both enabled and sponsored its promulgation. Rather
than compete with this brand of honesty or friendship, we
work to forge our own.

2. Commentate but Don't Pass Judgment

To our adolescents, even a passive observation on our parts
can be construed as a negative judgment. This is especially
true when we broach the sacrosanct subject of friendships.
The beauty of a peer friendship lies strictly in the eyes of the
beholder, despite other, especially parental, views or perspectives. So how do we convey our concerns about a friendship
without driving our adolescents further into its potentially

harmful (we fear) clutches? How do we determine when to encourage and/or discourage one of the most essential means of survival for our adolescents: an abiding friend?

US: *Was it fun having a friend along on the trip?*
THEM: *Yeah, it was great.*
US: *Do you think he had fun?*
THEM: *Yeah. He seemed to.*
US: *It was hard for us to tell; he didn't say much. He barely even said thank you and never offered to help. Did you notice that?*
THEM: *Yeah, I guess. He did with me, though. We talked a lot.*
US: *Is he just shy or do you think we intimidated him somehow?*
THEM: *Not sure. He's sorta quiet.*
US: *What did you guys talk about?*
THEM: *Everything.*
US: *Would you say he's pretty experienced?*
THEM: *What do you mean?*
US: *I mean with girls, or experimenting.*
THEM: *You mean likes alcohol or drugs? Here you go again . . .*
US: *I don't mean to assume anything, but when you spend four days with someone and they barely utter a word or look you in the eye, it's hard to know what to think. I need your help understanding him.*
THEM: *Look, he's a good kid. He goes over to his neighbor's house every day after school and plays with their blind son until his mom gets home from work. Last week, when Toby was really depressed, he got him to go talk to a teacher. He gets great grades and has really good instincts.*

*That's why I like him. Why do you always think I hang
out with juvenile delinquents?*
US: *I'm so glad to know all that about him. Listening to
your description, he reminds me of you. That's all great
stuff.*

We swallow the *I wish you had told me this earlier* thought
and let the compliment stand on its own.

There is no such thing as a missed opportunity to adjust
our reactions. When assessing the impact or influence of a
friend in our adolescents' lives, make the queries, even report
any interesting observations. Just try to avoid sounding too
sour.

Effective parenting depends on starting small and ending
small. Amid the madding cry for independence, it's up to us to
find and concatenate the recurring themes we hear from our
adolescents. That's the only way we'll know whom they're really listening to, and what they're really hearing. If we look
first, maybe we won't even have to leap to any wrong conclusions.

3. Get to Know Their Friends and, if Possible, Their Friends' Parents

The best way to know our adolescents' friends is to make
them welcome. This means refraining from psychological
frisking or negative commentary regardless of the characters
or costumes on display. For most of us, getting to know our
adolescents' friends means creating the opportunity to observe them in action, listen to their methods of persuasion,
and assess their influence. Unfortunately, these observations
are difficult to snatch from our mostly brief encounters.

The alternative—an open, or even qualified, invitation policy—entails obligation and work, both of which add weight to our already overburdened shoulders. The rewards can be great, however, especially when compared with the sacrifices. Let's review some of the benefits—and their costs—of opening up our homes in order to get to know our adolescents' friends. (Maybe if we all shared the burden, and any important findings, we could lessen each other's load.)

REWARD: Seeing them in action; knowing who's who in the friendship zoo.

SACRIFICES/REQUIREMENTS: We're more home-bound, whenever their friends are there, and more precautionary when we're not. The vast majority of problems arise when we're not home and don't make the necessary arrangements to prevent spontaneous gatherings in our absence (say, by leaving the house unwatched, even if our kids are supposed to be elsewhere). It takes only one cell phone call to trigger a stampede.

REWARD: Getting to know their friends, and dispelling preconceived (often negative) notions.

SACRIFICES/REQUIREMENTS: As parental hosts, we end up entertaining a variety of characters, some more savory than others. Depending upon our motivation and level of interest (opposite gender, a new favorite friend), we may want to create situations that allow for deeper insight, such as dinner invitations or even weekends away. Sometimes bigger investments yield higher dividends—especially in a world where we never even meet many of our adolescents' peers because they enter our teenagers' lives by way of nearly impossible-to-monitor text messages, Facebook-type Wall postings, and/or cell phones that we can't answer.

....

REWARD: Peace of mind; knowing where they are, what they're doing, and that they're safe.
SACRIFICES/REQUIREMENTS: Wear and tear on our homes—and us. (Which we can limit by designating or donating a confined, if small, space—and demanding respect for that space.)

....

REWARD: Our rules prevail; we define the parameters and set the limits. We know whom to trust and respect and whom not to (including our own adolescents).
SACRIFICES/REQUIREMENTS: Willingness to set *and* enforce responsible house rules that include abiding by and respecting both school rules and the law. For our adolescents' sakes, *we* communicate and enforce and let them reinforce. That may mean asking their friends to leave water bottles, knapsacks, or any other potential repositories for contraband, as well as car keys, at the door.

Especially when they're younger, this also means laying ground rules about open doors, lights, and the like. And it may mean temptation-proofing the house, such as limiting entrances and exits except across adult paths, or barring access to bedrooms and other isolated areas that could lead to unsafe behaviors. Of course, some teenagers will opt out of coming to a "sober" house. In response, we try to make it rewarding for those who do (see next Reward).

REWARD: The fun. Their respect. Fond memories that last—for them and us.

SACRIFICES/REQUIREMENTS: Let it be fun. This doesn't require the latest surround sound and an in-house soda fountain; it requires some basic essentials, such as a sincere welcome, respect for their privacy and independence, and, of course, some *simple* but appealing snacks!

Though never the life of the party, we need to be a presence. Start with a greeting ritual: friendly but direct eye contact and even a physical hug, pat, or handshake for each person entering the home turf, whether the gathering takes place inside or outside. If greeting someone new or suspect, make sure to be a presence, albeit unobtrusive. The easiest and most subtle way to glide in and out of the adolescent scene itself is via the food express (nothing fancy). This also happens to be the most direct route to everyone's heart, so keep those check-ins-disguised-as-deliveries coming. With each delivery, again make eye contact with whoever is in reach, and ask a benign (but informed) question: *Heard you won the game yesterday. Were they a tough team?* or *I think this is the first time you've been here. Did someone show you where the bathroom [or phone, or trash can] is?* These brief but pointed encounters afford us a moment to linger—and discreetly survey—for as long as feels natural. If doubt arises, pursue it with your adolescent privately: *I'm concerned that Morgan has some vodka with him. Can you check it out? If not, I'll have to.*

At the sound, or even hint, of a house rule breaking, discreetly lure those involved (including our own, whether under suspicion or not) out of earshot. State the concern, and don't be afraid to pose a direct question.

If a transgression occurs, the call should be clear and the consequences understood. No surprises. Dispassionate clarity both exhibits and demands respect.

When in doubt, force yourself to trust them. Respect goes two ways. Most adolescents choose friends who are more similar to themselves than different.

Of course, some adolescents, by their nature, prefer to enshroud themselves in a veil of privacy or secrecy impermeable, at least to adults. Penetrating this, or any, adolescent façade sometimes requires additional creative measures. As our adolescents float in and out of a series of peer-populated concentric circles, like nomads in search of a comfortable resting place, our mission remains to safeguard and protect. As one of many preventive measures, we band together with other parents and adults to form a chain of connections that hopefully extends the full circumference of our adolescents' territory. Held together with any available links (e-mail, phone, informal gatherings, or planned meetings), we rely on this chain to keep us all in direct and easy contact should the need arise. While some will use it frequently to monitor their adolescents' meanderings, others will rely on it only as a last resort. Regardless, isn't it better to know we're not alone in our surveillance? Isn't it reassuring that we have somewhere to turn in case we temporarily lose touch?

4. Know What We Need to Know

Despite admonishments to recede rather than intercede, our parenting responsibilities entitle us to many rights and privileges. While claiming those privileges is important, we often dread the ensuing confrontations—sometimes even to the point of dereliction of duty. We are well within our rights to require safety-related information, regardless of the time or place, but we may overstep the bounds by pressing too hard for details outside the purview of the Rules of Play.

Respect is another privilege (though not a right) to which we are entitled, but it must be earned. We do that in part by listening to and acknowledging our adolescents' opinions, even if we disagree with them. Remember, from their very first utterances, we are largely responsible for helping our adolescents find and develop their range of convictions. To belittle or ignore their voices (or those of their peers) insults not only their intelligence but our role as parents as well. On the other hand, careful listening solidifies the bond of mutual respect. Once earned, respect can transform what might otherwise be interpreted as intrusive demands into normal expectations, such as neatness, concern for their welfare—or that of others—or noise control.

5. In the Connection-Separation Tug-of-War—Yield First

As long as yielding doesn't endanger them. As long as yielding doesn't lead to decision gridlock or increase *our* ire. Yielding is cheap as long as it doesn't lead to cheap shots. A willingness to yield may actually lure our adolescents to stay in touch, a kind of giving in to get our way. Too often discounted or rejected as a sign of weakness, if done right, yielding can demonstrate unexpected strength.

> **US:** *What do you think the risks are of going with this group of friends, many of whom you've haven't hung with that much?*
> **THEM:** *What do you mean risks? Why is this risky?*
> **US:** *Well, I just don't know these kids very well. I wondered whether you had thought it all through?*

TRANSLATION: *I'm worried that this group of friends may lead you into unfamiliar or uncharted territory. Have you thought about how you would handle that?*

Since neither they nor we can predict what might happen, we can only plant seeds of anticipation in the hope of germinating preparedness.

THEM: *Nothing bad is going to happen! I promise!*
US: *As you know, my job is to worry about you staying safe. Your job is to make the right decisions to keep yourself safe. So call in like we agreed, or sooner if you need us. And have fun!*

The passage from childhood into adulthood, otherwise known as adolescence, can seem endless. And once through, there is no turning back (not that we'd want to). For some, the expedition is fraught with wrong turns and mishaps, maybe worse. For others, the journey is shorter, more straightforward. In the company of a wide assortment of peers, our adolescents test and rely, reject and are rejected. In the end, the friends they emerge with invariably wear the values we all recognize, and the fit between their world and ours feels much more comfortable.

Without friends, our adolescents cast about in a sea of loneliness. Friends provide the frames of reference, the benchmarks, the testing ground. While we won't always approve of or like the nature of the tests, the alternative is isolation, which can lead to stunted growth or worse. We learned by using the buddy system. We know it works.

WHEN WE SAY *NO*, THEY HEAR *MAYBE*

NOT SURPRISINGLY, THERE ARE THINGS OUR ADOLESCENTS know that we don't—and things they know that they don't know they know. (A good example is our adolescents' uncanny ability to tell when a *no* really means *maybe*.) More important than our knowing *what* they know is our knowing *how they think about* what they know. To think clearly is to choose clearly. And a clear choice means that more than one perspective has informed an action.

The ability to recognize another perspective marks the beginning of a new leg of our teenagers' pilgrimage to adulthood. Suddenly paths not seen, or perhaps noticed, open up, leading the way to viewpoints other than their own. From these new levels of reasoning, risks sometimes appear smaller than they really are—but then again, so do the challenges. Unaware of their already overloaded brain circuitry, our adolescents struggle to order their chaotic worlds by segmenting the many, often conflicting influences that vie for their attention. Hence, they lean even more heavily on their peers for support, and teachers, coaches, and clergy for knowledge and mentorship. But, as always, they look to us for direction. Directions that distinguish the right way from the wrong, the smooth roads from the bumpy—and the pitfalls in between. If we have positioned ourselves well, we remain stationed in the back of their minds, their moral compasses, ready for action. Let's explore how that might work.

REALITY BYTES

NO MATTER HOW TIGHT THE ADULT SUPERVISION, THE REIGN of most childhood playgrounds belongs to the children themselves. And somehow the implicit rules of childhood fraternity forbid any victims to clue us in on the elaborate politics of the power cliques or the brutal bullies. By adolescence, these playgrounds expand well beyond an enclosed, relatively safe set of structures. Once again, our children-turned-adolescents grant us only glimpses of their victories and defeats, and the origins and extent of any battle wounds, either inflicted or incurred. So we gather information however, wherever we can.

Despite a steady flow of studies on all facets of adolescence, from oral sex to STDs to buying patterns, many of us prefer not to acknowledge just how close to home some of these teen trends may hit. Instead, we tend to throw up roadblocks disguised as rules and censorship disguised as constraints, hoping that if a potential harm is out of *our* sight, it must be out of *their* minds. Since the average American (which includes most of our adolescents) sees more than twenty thousand sexual acts, references, and innuendos annually—on TV alone[1]—we may be fighting a losing battle.

A recent study found that by twelfth grade, three out of four adolescents are drinking regularly and are sexually active;

almost half of them are also doing drugs. (These statistics, by the way, are higher among affluent families, and especially with boys—for whom drinking, particularly in younger adolescence, is more directly associated with status: 28 percent of boys versus 6 percent of girls.[2]) But that's twelfth grade, we might argue, by which time their values groundwork is already laid. Okay, then consider another study, which shows a steady increase in drinking, beginning in the sixth grade with 16 percent. This number then jumps to 57 percent by the ninth grade and 71 percent by the tenth. Eighty-two percent of twelfth graders report drinking alcohol regularly.[3] That equates to roughly 70 percent of *all* high schoolers. A different study found that one out of five fourteen-year-olds and one-third of fifteen-year-old girls admit to having had sex (compared with less than 5 percent in 1970), as do 45 percent of fifteen-year-old boys.[4]

Before assigning a *Does Not Apply to Me* (or my adolescent) label on the above data, note that research shows that 90 percent of mothers who think their kids are having sex are right, whereas those who think their kids are *not* having sex are wrong *50 percent* of the time.[5] Whether our adolescents are or are not, they face the same questions, issues, and temptations. They chase questions in search of answers and know when our talk doesn't match our walk.

For those seeking the *why* data, a study on teen drinking cited social isolation and academic pressure as the primary reasons that 30 percent of tenth graders reported getting "completely drunk" within the past year, and one out of three used illicit substances.[6] Similarly, a corroborating study reported boredom, access to twenty-five dollars or more, and high stress as the primary reasons that adolescents smoke, drink alcohol, and use illicit drugs.[7] Though these reasons should not be new, the real question is: Which, if any, apply to us? A majority of the parents interviewed for this study said that it was unrealistic to expect that their adolescents would never use drugs. The same probably holds true for our expectations regarding sex.

Ask postadolescents (those, say, in their early twenties living primarily out of the house) in a direct and nonthreatening way to reflect on high school antics involving risky behaviors, and they will most likely corroborate the above findings. Given the odds that most of our adolescents will end up venturing into some unsafe territory or other, the point is less *how young?* than *how will they deal?* Which begs the question: How far out of the loop are we and do we want to be?

Values Clarification

HOW MANY OF OUR ADOLESCENTS WOULD BE ABLE TO EXPLIC-itly define not their own, but *our* values regarding sex, drugs, and alcohol? If asked to articulate them ourselves, in the company of our adolescents, how clearly and comprehensibly could *we* do so? Reassuringly, 82 percent of parents believe that they are good models. Sadly, only 60 percent of adolescents agree.[8]

If not ours, then whose job is it to make sure that our adolescents are absolutely certain where the indelible, irrefutable line is between respectful and disrespectful—and safe and unsafe—behaviors, and why? And while it may be up to our adolescents to know where the line is and to not cross over it, it's up to us to draw it—and keep its borders visible. Yes, there are health classes and clergy and other responsible sources to reinforce our work. But it is *our* job to keep them safe, nourished, and sheltered. Light sockets and matches and street crossings were then. Drugs and alcohol and sex are now.

So are lying and stealing and cheating. When was the last time we checked our paths for any inconsistencies or hypocrisies that may have inadvertently spilled when we stumbled over a response or opted to say rather than do? By not posting our values like traffic signs along their way, we risk leaving them stranded on a hundred different moral street corners. Better that they learn to navigate using our signage than someone else's.

> **THEM:** *Jemm's coming over to watch* Gossip Girl.
> **US:** *Oh? Tell me why you like that show so much.*

When an adolescent fad takes hold, we'd best learn more about it, especially those that lay bare all of the quintessentially primal but no longer private urges of today's teenagers.

> **THEM:** *Same stuff. Boys, girls, and relationships.*
> **US:** *You mean boys, girls, and sex? What is it about these shows?* [Showing disapproval through humor is okay as long as it doesn't disable the point.]
> **THEM:** *I like them. They're funny! Remember, you watched it, even liked it!*
> **US:** *Yes, I did. Mostly, I was embarrassed for the dad. Remind me again about the relationships—who's involved with whom? I know that the one couple broke up and the girl starts dating the best friend's former boyfriend. So are they still together?* [Engage, don't judge. A thought process can be a revelation unto itself.]
> **THEM:** *I know you think just because I like watching these shows, I'm going to act the way they do! I'm not!*
> **US:** *What worries me most is how getting trashed excuses irresponsible behavior, and relationships are defined in terms of how fast kids can get to intercourse.*

THEM: *Whatever . . .*

US: *Do you agree?*

THEM: *No!*

US: *I know you love these shows. I need to know that you are at least thinking about what you're seeing. So you name some risks that it ignores, and you'll at least be getting closer to a yes regarding Jemm coming over.*

THEM: *Look, I know what the risks are. You've told me and I've learned about them in school.*

US: *Okay, then name one. Just one.*

THEM: *Geez . . . this is so lame . . .* [or some such sanitized adolescent expletive] *unwanted pregnancy, STDs, responsibility. Stuff like that. Okay?*

US: *What about the psychological risks?*

THEM: *What?*

US: *The much more common risks that occur all the time, like hurt, remorse, jealousy, shame. The ones that don't get talked about, but are just as hurtful.*

THEM: *Get off my case, okay? You're acting like I'm a criminal or something. I just want to watch a TV show!*

US: *Okay. Here's the deal. After you've seen it, you need to be able to tell me what you think the moral of the episode is in a way that I* [that is, a parent/adult] *can understand. Okay? That's the deal. Take it or leave it.*

THEM: *You can't stop me; I'll just watch it online some other time.*

US: *You're right, I can't monitor everything you do online, but you either recognize the benefits of mutual trust, or you don't. That trust buys you a lot of things you want, from cell phones to freedom. It's also part of Showing Respect. . . .*

[Sound a little like an ultimatum? It shouldn't. It should sound like Keeping in Touch.]

Remember, the name of the game is to keep the conversation going. To ensure this, the ball is always in our court. So, we impart our values like trade secrets that they can use in times of trial.

THE GREAT (ADOLESCENT)
PARENTING INHIBITORS

ONE OF OUR BIGGEST PARENTING OBSTACLES MAY BE OUR own reluctance. Perhaps we are reluctant to relinquish our role as gatekeepers of what they see and do. Perhaps we are reluctant to expose our own ambivalence, lest it be contagious. Perhaps we are reluctant to weigh in too heavily, lest we drive them away. Perhaps we are simply not comfortable with the language of sex or drugs or explanations, so we leave that to others more adept or fluent. But we can only fool them for so long. The longer we wait, the more we have to lose, usually in the form of credibility and respect.

Along our parenting way, it is easy to trip over our own embarrassment and concern. Embarrassment, however painful, usually strikes quickly and then fades, sometimes leaving us exposed but not altered. (For some tips on overcoming the embarrassment of talking with our adolescents, see chapter 3, Controlling Them Is Not the Point.) Other times, however, our embarrassments expose the fact that we reflect a past that no longer exists. And no matter how vivid our memories, our adolescents often view our pasts as faded fairy tales, sometimes poignant, often outgrown. Take a recent finding that only 28 percent of adolescents feel embarrassed to admit to their own virginity, yet 48 percent of adults find such an admission embarrassing.[9] What more vivid illustration of the impact of growing up in a different era, where AIDS and teen pregnancy are both household fears? What better illustration that regardless of how closely our adolescents may resemble us, they often don't reflect us.

Concern, on the other hand, has a much more complex root system that preys on our deepest vulnerabilities. Most of the time, we bear our concerns rationally, relying on them to trigger a second look—or an alarm. Concerns about rejection or looking foolish invade us like parasites, sometimes draining our patience and/or distorting our perspectives. Still, it's the heavier, or irrational, concerns that threaten to impede our parenting progress. The heaviest and most irrational of all our concerns, of course, is that some horrific catastrophe will befall our children. That one bad decision, or break, that in one split second permanently shatters a still-young and fragile lifetime. This overriding concern for our children's welfare sets in at the conception of our own parenthood and subsequently threatens to sabotage our rationality if and when it gets too close.

A less terrifying but no less prevalent concern pertains to our adolescents' acquisition of knowledge, as if certain types of knowledge can and will bollix our carefully constructed circuitry of *dos* and *dont's,* like a computer virus. *Plenty of literature substantiates that exposure can normalize behaviors, leading to increased occurrence.* A recent study posits that TV violence alone runs the same risk for increases in aggressive behavior as smoking does for increases in cancer.[10] No matter how foolproof our protection devices, the fact remains that children understand the major role that sex, drugs, and alcohol play in our culture as early as eight or nine. Like it or not, believe it or not, the data in this book, and elsewhere, strongly suggest that our adolescents already know much more than we tell them about sex and drinking and drugs. In fact, often they are the ones telling *us.*

We can no more strain the impurities from the information

that constantly deluges the adolescent brain than we can disinfect the impure thoughts that form as a result. So we either leave them to unscramble the myriad messages they receive from a multitude of unreliable sources, or we attempt to clarify these messages. Truth rarely harms an adolescent. (That doesn't mean we have to tell them everything. But we need to talk to them constantly, and what we *do* tell them has to be the truth.)

> **US:** *So why do you think that Sadie had oral sex with him?*
> **THEM:** *Cuz! It's no big deal. Lots of kids do it.*
> **US:** *But you said they're not even in a relationship.*
> **THEM:** *They're not.*
> **US:** *So did they talk about whether the other wanted to do it? Or did they just go for it?*
> **THEM:** *They're just friends. They do it for fun.*
> **US:** *So how did she feel afterward?*
> **THEM:** *Fine.*
> **US:** *You know how easy it is for girls, even more than boys, to get labeled. Is she worried about that?*
> **THEM:** *Mom, nobody cares! Anyway, she said she wouldn't have done it if he had asked. He didn't, so it was up to her. It was her decision!*

How many of us focus our discussions about sexuality on how to say *no*, rather than how to communicate about what each person wants or doesn't want to do? Staving off carnal pleasures has challenged human nature ever since Adam and Eve. So although the ability to say *no* effectively is critical, we might also consider that they may not always want to choose it. And then what?

US: *Actually, it takes two to decide, which means engaging in oral sex should be a conscious and mutual decision and not just something that feels right at the moment.*

THEM: *Well, they both wanted to. You think oral sex only goes one way. It doesn't. Most of the time, the girls are getting it, too. They're both into it.*

US: *If two people believe that they are ready to engage in that level of sex, I just hope they are ready and willing to talk about condoms and STDs, and how they will feel when a "friend with benefits" gets a real girl- or boyfriend. Do you think they were actually that ready?*

THEM: *Why do you have to make everything into such a big deal?*

Note: Don't expect, or push for, an answer to every question. And don't assume that they don't hear us just because they don't answer. If compelled to satisfy the need to know, try something like, *Just nod if you heard me.* Otherwise, leave it. One healthy serving of values per discussion is probably enough . . .

Given our insider status, we can scarcely afford to forgo the opportunity to record the original soundtracks in our areas of concern, particularly out of our own reluctance or embarrassment. If our stances are clear, the tracks will replay over and over, like the chorus to an old song that still rings true.

OUR MORAL ADDRESSES

BY ADOLESCENCE, OUR CHILDREN START TOTING A MENTAL backpack full of fears and questions, unsure where to put many of them or which ones to keep hidden. Many of us may just be reawakening from a long hiatus from such questions as

*When is it okay/not okay to smoke a joint, have sex [*other than with our spouses*], ride with illegal drivers* or *drive when we've had one too many?* We might not even notice our adolescents carrying a heavier worry load. Few adolescents truly shun our attention even as they squirm under its perceived intensity. So unless we listen intently to both their verbal and nonverbal cues, we may never know where to steer the conversation. Chances are if we don't ask, they'll never tell. (And even then, they'll never tell us everything. See chapter 2, Truth Is as Malleable as Their Friday Night Plans.) Just remember, it takes two to tango—and have a conversation. We just want to be one of the two.

To better understand and guide our adolescents, it is useful to calibrate our own values to the kinds of situations they face on a regular basis. One way to do that is to focus on three particularly pertinent (*how,* not *what*) questions:

- What do we really know about how *our adolescents* might respond in a given (tempting) situation?
- Do we know how *we* might respond if we discover some undesirable truths about our teenagers?
- What do our adolescents think *actually* goes on with their peers in that same situation?

The point here is to assess what we do and don't know both about our adolescents *and* ourselves. Only then can we understand how they think about what they know. Only then can we aim our conversations accurately. Only then can we really claim to be *in touch.*

The more vague our messages about what constitutes sex or drugs or alcohol, or for that matter stealing or lying, the easier they are to ignore. (Remember first to assess and acknowledge our own culpabilities. For example, do we omit or obfuscate information, drink before we drive, and so on?) If, however, our adolescents are clear that we consider oral sex to be sex (or not) and one beer, regardless of the circumstances, to be as potentially dangerous as three (or not), then they know what qualifies as fair play (or not).

THE *KNOW WHAT WE KNOW* ASSESSMENT

Using the scale below as a guide, rate your knowledge, with a 5 indicating *high degree of knowledge*, down to a 1 meaning *don't know at all. They* = our teenagers; *we* = us.

a. They really like someone who wants to have sex with them, but are not sure whether to go ahead with it. What do we know about:
  i.   How they would respond?
  ii. How we would respond if they did?
  iii. What do they think really happens with peers in the same situation?

We know   5   4   3   2   1   *We don't know*

  Is it different at age fifteen than at sixteen? Or seventeen? Or eighteen?
  Is it different for boys than for girls?

b. They have been in a committed relationship with the same person (whom we also really like) for six months or longer. What do we know about:
  i.   How they would respond to:
      Petting—oral sex—genital touching—intercourse?
  ii. How we would respond if they engaged in one or more of these activities?

iii. What do they think really happens with peers in the same situation?

We know   5   4   3   2   1   *We don't know*

Is it different at age fifteen than at sixteen? Or seventeen? Or eighteen?
Is it different if they have been involved with the person for less than six months?

c. They are home alone and bored. An opposite-gender friend calls and wants to come over to "fool around" (also known as a *friend with benefits*). What do we know about:
   i.   How they would respond?
   ii. How we would respond if they engaged in this kind of casual sex?
   iii. What do they think really happens with peers in the same situation?

We know   5   4   3   2   1   *We don't know*

Is it different if they have been in a previous relationship with the person?
Is it different at age fourteen than at fifteen? Or sixteen?

d. They are attending a special event or family celebration and are offered some alcohol. What do we know about:
   i.   How they would respond to the offer to drink:
        Wine—beer—hard lemonade (5.2 percent alcohol)—hard liquor?
   ii. How we would respond if they did?
   iii. What do they think really happens with peers in the same situation?

We know   5   4   3   2   1   *We don't know*

Is it different at age fifteen than at sixteen? Or seventeen? Or eighteen?

Is one serving different from two? How about three?
Is it different for boys than for girls?

e. They go to a party where parents are away and alcohol is present. What do we know about:
 i. How they would respond to the offer to drink:
 Wine—beer—hard lemonade (5.2 percent alcohol)—hard
 liquor?
 ii. How we would respond if they did?
 iii. What do they think really happens with peers in the same
 situation?

We know   5   4   3   2   1   *We don't know*

Is it different at age fifteen than at sixteen? Or seventeen? Or
eighteen?
Is one beer different from two? How about three?
Is it different for boys than for girls?

f. They go to a party where the parents are home and alcohol is
present. What do we know about:
 i. How our adolescents would respond to the offer of:
 Marijuana—prescription drugs (Valium, sleeping pills, stimu-
 lants)—cocaine, or other hard drugs?
 ii. How we would respond?
 iii. What do they think really happens with peers in the same situation?

We know   5   4   3   2   1   *We don't know*

Is it different at age fifteen than at sixteen? Or seventeen? Or
eighteen?
Is marijuana different from another drug? Which one(s)?
Is it different for boys than for girls?

The purpose of this self-assessment is to lead us on a tour of our own opinions so we can more clearly guide our adolescents.

The less certain we are about what *our adolescents* think, what *we* think, and what *they* think *we* think, the more we may need to probe the origins or motivations of our opinions and how we impart them. If we're clear about what we *and* they believe and value, no matter how wide the gulf, we know where to focus our conversations.

An important aspect of this assessment, besides pointing out any discrepancies between what we do and don't know about what and how we *and* our adolescents think, is that not one item in it is far-fetched. Not *one.* For most of our adolescents, these situations reflect their reality. So regardless of what we believe, or want our adolescents to believe, there are things that they know about—if not do—that they will never tell us.

Although control over our adolescents is not the point, conversation is. So we take what we can get, even the raw-edged raps that keep us tuned in to their adolescent thought channels.

GENDER BALANCING

ONE OF THE MURKIEST AREAS OF ADOLESCENT DEVELOPMENT belongs to gender expectations. The age-old dilemma of adjustable standards based on gender still plagues many a parent–adolescent conversation. Although much has been written about the distinguishing characteristics, merging sensibilities, and heightened expectations of both adolescent boys and girls, many of our parenting decisions remain stuck on one side or the other of a gender gap. But the mixed messages don't just come from us. From the classroom to the playing fields, from television ads to the mating habits of their favorite stars, our adolescents field enough contradictions to confound a politician.

A *New York Times* article sketched a new breed of empowered, or macho, girl.[11] Following in the gender-equality-seeking, sexual-mores-questioning footsteps that many of us helped forge, this new age adolescent feminist easily separates sex from love. Otherwise, she risks relinquishing the control she has been taught to assert by us and by a multitude of modern societal models and images. Few women achieve today's pinnacles of success, whether in show or some other line of business, without working harder than their male counterparts. Fortunately, these achievements are beginning to garner more recognition than ever before. After all, don't we want our adolescent daughters to believe that they can achieve at comparable levels to our sons? Should we be surprised if they also want more power in matters of love and sex? Or are we still imparting that—whether or not we believe or practice(d) it ourselves—sex without love equals promiscuity (a label that may be desirable to some but positive to very few)?

Is the macho girl promiscuous, or just assertive? Perhaps, unwittingly, our adolescents have added a new dimension to the good girl–bad girl discussion. This dimension defines girls not by their willingness to "put out," but by their willingness to demand equal power. Imagine if, rather than instilling fear in our daughters that all boys want is sex, we instill their right to assert *what* they want, *when* they want it—and not be considered a prude or a slut yet still be desirable and respected.

Not many girls, past the tomboy stage, risk revealing too much of their masculine sides. Few adolescent boys ever risk revealing *any* of their feminine traits. Instead, boys and girls fit themselves so tightly into a prescribed gender mold that they often cut off the circulation to less familiar, thus less comfortable, aspects of their personalities. If our adolescent girls and boys weren't bound by so many preexisting stereotypes of what they should and shouldn't be thinking, feeling, doing, sexually and otherwise, then the one out of five female adolescents who experience date-related sexual violence in high school might feel empowered to prevent such aggressions.[12]

Have we drawn a clear enough distinction for our adolescents between *being* anything they want and *doing* anything they want? According to a survey of adult women, half of all rape victims are under eighteen.[13] And a recent study by the Center for Disease Control reports that 11.3 percent of girls and 4.5 percent of boys were forced to have intercourse.[14]

Perhaps our daughters aren't sure about the difference between looking sexy and wanting (or not wanting) to engage in sex. Perhaps our sons long for intimacy as much as girls do.

Adolescent boys grapple with their own assortment of incompatible pressures, even if their facial hair and lowered voices imply prowess and competence. First, the adolescent male must find a way to dispel his fear of failure, which means finding a girlfriend, or at least a willing girl, while remaining sensitive and respectful of her wishes. Second, he must figure out how to "be a man" in the eyes of male counterparts, and us, all while staying safe, all amid relentless hormonal urges. Third, he must stake his position as participant, observer, player, or some combination thereof in the myriad bravado games staged by male counterparts, without opening himself up to ridicule or rumor. Worst of all, to which of these groups—peers? girls? adults?—can he confide his doubts and insecurities without appearing weak? So we keep our eyes out for even the smallest opportunities to release some of this pressure on our sons.

> **US:** *What would you say if a girl wanted to do something you didn't feel comfortable doing?*
> **THEM:** *I don't know. Give me a break. Why do you have to ask these kinds of questions!*
> **US:** *What if she told you she loved you?*
> **THEM:** *We are not having this conversation!*
> **US:** *C'mon, what would you say?*
> **THEM:** *Well, obviously it would depend on whether I loved her back, wouldn't it?*
> **US:** *What if you thought you did?*
> **THEM:** *Then why would I be uncomfortable?*
> **US:** *Because it could be confusing. If she told you she loved you, you might think you really did love her back. Because maybe you weren't looking for the real signs.*
> **THEM:** *What real signs?*

While many of our adolescents might use sarcasm to mask their discomfort with this kind of conversation, others let down their guards cautiously. Not to be deterred, especially if they are still in the same room with us, we press on.

> **US:** *Like whether you and she both feel comfortable doing something, which is different from feeling physically aroused.*
> **THEM:** *I have no idea what you're talking about.*
> **US:** *I guess I'm just talking about a consultation with your conscience—and with her. Is this really what you both want—or just you—or just her? Or maybe things have gone far enough—at least for now.*

THEM: *I doubt I'm going to be uncomfortable, so don't worry about it.*

US: *A lot of times, especially in the heat of the moment, it's hard to distinguish between feeling comfortable and feeling good. Do you think you could tell if a girl was uncomfortable with what you were doing?*

THEM: *Of course . . . I guess . . . I assume she'd say . . .*

US: *But what if she didn't? Do you think you could tell?*

THEM: *Look, it's up to her to say. I'm not a mind reader. Most girls I know would say. Of course, if she said she wasn't comfortable, I'd stop.*

US: *Sex can get very confusing because sometimes your body speaks louder than your mind. It's probably best always to ask her if it's okay before you move from kissing to petting or from petting to the next step. It's as much your responsibility to make sure she's comfortable as it is hers to say so.*

THEM: *Why? It's her body. Is it her decision to make sure I'm comfortable?*

US: *Absolutely. Sex, above all, is about mutual commitment and consent. That means taking responsibility both in terms of safety and in terms of respect—and not just for you but also for the other person. The Rules of Play apply here, too!*

Maybe the fact that the terms *gender* and *sex* get used interchangeably is no accident. The term *intimacy,* however, carries neither a sexual nor a gender bias. Built on respect, trust, and acceptance, we associate the term *intimacy* with more gender-neutral, mature feelings. For some, sex is to intimacy what popularity is to friendship. They think they need one to get to the other. In our society, sex is easily joked about, poked fun at, taken for granted. Intimacy is not. Perhaps the conversation could start there.

HOW TO DEAL

1. Take a clear stand.

2. Make sure that *no* doesn't mean *maybe*.

3. Teach them to think; the right actions will follow.

4. Be prepared for the unforeseen byproducts.

1.Take a Clear Stand

Perhaps the best offer we can make to our adolescents is to be their moral compass, always pointing in the right direction, always available, unwavering. But to be effective, we must also be easily readable, our orientation clear and unequivocal. Otherwise, we contribute to their confusion and even risk hampering their search for themselves.

Despite earnest attempts to communicate with them, why does the data show that most adolescents won't actually call home (85 percent) to ask for a ride if under the influence?[15] Could it be that they don't really understand our mix of messages, or trust our reaction in the face of disappointment? Maybe this data is evidence that just saying the words *no questions asked* doesn't adequately or honestly reveal or convey our true feelings, values, and beliefs about risky or uncondoned behaviors. Sure, we say we'll pick them up, but then what? Is it humanly, let alone parentally, possible to refrain from an inquisition or castigation? What if they had a great time drinking and plan to do it again? What if they *want* to have sex and believe they *are* ready?

THEM: *But what if it feels right and I really like him [or her]?*

US: *In this family, we view sex as a very important part of a relationship. This means it is part of a commitment you make to a person and not just something fun to do when you like someone. That's the difference between sex and intimacy.*

THEM: *Look, you're blowing this way out of proportion. Hooking up is no big deal. Of course kids do it for fun. You've said yourself: Sex is important and wonderful.*

US: *As part of an intimate relationship, not a casual friendship. We still disapprove of oral sex and intercourse at your age for all the reasons I just described* [try to be as literal as possible; they certainly are]*, but if you choose to go against our wishes, then above all you need to be safe. This means taking the necessary precautions. So as long as you know where we stand, also know that we will always help you stay safe.*

Anticipating the *Yeah, right* that they're thinking, we explain . . .

US: *What I mean is, if you've made the decision that you need birth control, and you want help getting it, I'll help.*

Does it sound contradictory to convey disapproval and then enable our teenagers by providing assistance? The answer is: It's complicated. A recent survey of both adolescents and parents presented the following scenario to both groups:

US: *I don't want you to have sex. In fact, not having sex is the only certain way to avoid pregnancy and STDs. But*

*if you do end up having sex, be certain to use birth control
or protection.*

All were then asked the question: Does this message encourage sex? Seventy-five percent of the adolescents and 64 percent of the parents said *No*.[16]

So we keep repeating the question (to ourselves and to our adolescents): *What do we most care about?* We then answer with the mantra: *That you stay safe, show respect, keep in touch.* Once again, a recent study reveals a disconnect between what *we* think our adolescents think and what *they* really think. Forty-five percent of adolescents attribute *us* with the greatest influence on their decisions to have sex. Yet only 32 percent of us regard our influence as primary. Conversely, 48 percent of parents assume that friends' influence outweighs ours, whereas 31 percent of adolescents confer the *greatest influence* distinction on their friends.[17]

We know (because we've been there) that fear of parental consequences drives many of the poor choices our adolescents make (like lying). Think about the implications of that. Does this mean we abolish all consequences? Of course not. But it might help the parent-adolescent conversation to establish a demilitarized zone: neutral ground where they can tell us any truth and they know we will listen; a place where mistakes can be vetted openly and are judged in accordance with the Rules of Play; a place where honesty is more important than guilt.

All the adolescent research shows that they look to our signals first. Displayed effectively, disapproval signals *stop* and encouragement signals *go*. The clearer these signals, the more embedded they become, like little internal alarms triggered by risk, demanding judgment. As many of us know, the laser-sharp tongue of an adolescent can easily pierce any argument not bolstered by an even stronger conviction. As often as possible, we hark back to the Rules of Play, reinforcing their importance, clarifying our positions, marking their boundaries:

- **Stay safe.** *If you drink alcohol, you are breaking the law . . . harming your brain . . . impairing your judgment . . . potentially jeopardizing others.*
- **Show respect.** *If you break your curfew . . . are rude . . . fail to do your schoolwork, chores, and so on, you are not respecting the rules we have established within this home and family.*
- **Keep in touch.** *If you don't let us know where you are going and what you are doing, we can't do our job, which is to flag danger and help keep you safe. Even if, someday soon, global positioning devices (GPS) will aid us in tracking our teenagers' whereabouts, that should not preclude their responsibility to keep in touch.*

Ultimately, the power to abide by the Rules of Play rests with them. Our power comes from securing their buy-in and holding them accountable. Our power comes from being clear.

2. Make Sure That *No* Doesn't Mean *Maybe*

As our adolescents emerge into the glare of the adult world, who do we hold up as the real heroes and heroines of our time? Paragons of courage? Models of honesty and respectability? Purveyors of peace? Do we point to world leaders who practice what they preach—or the government in general? How about the church? The venerable *New York Times* or *Wall Street Journal*? Public television? Do we point to sports figures? Business leaders? If asked about the influence of any of these arguable pillars of society, what might our adolescents say? Or what do we say about them, especially within earshot of our impressionable teens? Too often, they hear us comparing shock values like stock trades; they see us shrug off our own inability to keep harm at bay. It's our children's adolescence . . . do we know who their models are?

In the end, the politics of adolescence is local; therefore, it is up to us to provide the footsteps for them to follow. As a headmaster of a high school wrote in a letter to parents:

> *If there were something in the water supply that killed dozens of . . . teenagers every year, or there were a sniper picking off . . . high school students every couple of weeks, we wouldn't say that's just how it is. We would insist that some authority put a stop to these killings. In the matter of teenage drinking, that authority is parents.*[18]

Too often we loosen our grip on a resolute *no* as it oozes into a slippery *maybe* from which our adolescents deftly extract a lukewarm *yes*. And then resolve not to succumb to the same conditions—next time.

THEM: *But I didn't mean to . . .*

And they probably didn't. But they also know that the indiscretion probably won't cost much.

US: *Okay, then let's synchronize our watches. You tell me when, and I'll let you know whether that works for us. If not, we'll have to talk about what else needs to give.*

Friends change. So do teachers, coaches, clergy, other trusted advisers. For most adolescents, *we* represent the constant in their lives, the themes, the familiar refrains.

So when our adolescents look to us, what do they expect to see? They expect to see our face in the cheering crowd, invisible to all but them. They expect us always to be within earshot but never listening in. They expect us to find the lost sweatshirt or book or cell phone and know how it got there. They expect us to wait for them however long they may take. In other words, they expect us to be there, when the phone rings, when the question is asked, when the need arises. Always, like time ticking. And we try to live up to these expectations because of who we are and who we want them to be—with one possible exception: They expect *no* to mean *maybe* when it really should mean *no*.

3. Teach Them to Think; The Right Actions Will Follow

Being a parent doesn't make us a sage or even an expert. It doesn't guarantee that our answers are always right, nor that we have all of them all the time. Being a parent, however, does mean that we have made enough mistakes to learn from them, tested enough alternatives enough times to claim experience as an ally, and gained enough perspective on our results to share our wisdom. But we also recognize that wisdom can't be handed down, any more than a college degree or a job promotion can.

Drawing on our own storehouses, we introduce our adolescents to a vast array of tools, tirelessly demonstrating their use. Coping tools, respect tools, responsibility tools—we name each one for what it does and how it can help our adolescents think on their own. We provide endless opportunities for practice, marking their growing confidence by the frequency with which they can cite their own mistakes. As they gain confidence and competence, we up the ante by giving them more rein, more opportunity to hone new skills. We acknowledge each success as if it's their first. In other words, we teach them to use the most valuable set of tools they will ever possess: their thinking tools.

Most of us are good parents, most of the time. We provide shelter, keep our children safe, nurture them. For the most part, our adolescents cooperate, rewarding our efforts with sincere, if erratic, bursts of affection or humor or raw energy. When they forget, we hold them accountable, by invoking the Rules of Play. That's how we attempt to teach them to think before they act.

4. Be Prepared for the Unforeseen Byproducts

No sooner do we decipher an adolescent consuming trend, sometimes even joining as a better-late-than-never adopter, than a new one hurls at us so fast, we don't even see it coming. One such trend can be found in peer-to-peer webcam-based video chat cum game sites. A recent example, Chatroulette (created by a seventeen-year-old Russian boy), enables our adolescents to explore a universe of anonymous entries that look and feel both personal and entertaining. Free, so far, from legal or (much) parental oversight, adolescents log on and *click Next* their way from real kids playing everything from music to dress up, to lechers exposing themselves.

Occasionally, these trends, like sexting from texting, are aberrational outgrowths, already metastasized by the time we learn about them.

But once aware, we begin to decipher a steady flow of unsettling findings that threaten to drown what's left of any childhood innocence.

Of the one out of five adolescents who send inappropriate images across cyberwires, 40 percent claim that they feel forced into it.[19] Fifty-six percent of girls and 64 percent of boys admit to posting untruths online.[20] Small consolation that fourteen states are pursuing legislation that declares sexting a misdemeanor.[21]

Those who enter these worlds do so at their own risk and best that they check their feelings at the keyboard—or develop the callouses needed to stay in the game.

> **US:** *What other message might an image of a bare breast or penis sent across the Internet have to, let's say, an adult, who sees it out of context [*face straight, composure clenched*]?*
>
> **THEM:** *I told you, it was a mistake, I didn't mean to send it to you! It was a butt dial. Anyway, it was a joke! Of course, I didn't mean it.*
>
> **US:** *I understand what happened; it's happened to me too. But the issue is that the words you sent, "I want you inside me," whether you meant them or not, send a very graphic, not to mention disrespectful, message. You're lucky this came to me instead of a teacher or boss who also might be in your phone. The point is that you have to own not only what you do, but what you say, to whom you say it, and where else your messages might end up.*
>
> **THEM:** *But it was a joke…everybody gets that stuff happens.*
>
> **US:** *Yes, I get that. But the thing about these messages is you can't take them back. So imagine if . . .*

Some lessons hit their mark and we see the impact perk our adolescents up right before our eyes. Others seem to disappear, like water into soil, in search of a more dispersed purpose.

Without any "back in the day" context to draw on, it's

difficult for us to grasp the intensity of life uninterrupted by 24/7 opportunities to deliver a judgment, render a reaction, launch a repercussion. Renditions of a misdeed or misunderstanding, birthed in a school hallway, gather speed and ferocity as they penetrate the real-life barrier into cyberspace. And once an adolescent incident enters cyberdom, it can gather momentum with hurricane force and as much devastation. Always on the lookout for senseless cruelties, we talk about the havoc that cyberbullying or spreading rumors can wreak, the cowardice that belies lack of accountability or responsibility for one's actions. We point out, as cited in a recent *New York Times* article, that the Internet "records everything and forgets nothing."[22] And, as always, we call upon the Rules of Play. For the victims of such cruelty, we provide the calm, the harbor where our adolescents can always dock—just long enough to gather perspective, strength to stand by, and up for, those in need, be reminded that Showing Respect works both ways.

Another unforeseen byproduct of digital nativism relates to the writing habits of the impressionable adolescent. Fluency in the language of online writing comes easily to the unbridled adolescent, and once mastered, inextricably entwines with their thought processes until the two are as one. For us digital immigrants, situational writing styles are still first nature; we adapt accordingly. But for our fully textualized adolescents, the only difference between the written and the spoken word is one's physical proximity to the receiver, with texting sometimes still winning out over face-to-face conversation even when the receiver is within earshot. Sixty percent of adolescents view shorthand texting as "writing," and more incorporate this staccato style of writing into their school work. (Yet 86 percent believe that good writing is important to their success!).[23]

Many educators worry that truncation of the written

word is symptomatic of a larger shift in thought processes themselves. The search for knowledge that used to necessitate deeper and deeper dives into more and more complex realms has yielded to skimming, or power browsing.

Far from clean, the slate our adolescents learn to write on is more cluttered and muddled than ever before. Not just by the blur that separates the written from the spoken word but by the ethics that govern ownership in the free-for-all idea marketplace of the Internet. This kind of "free appropriation writing" has helped to springboard the notion of user-generated content into the mainstream, giving rise to the Wikipedia phenomenon, the twenty-first century's fountain of communal knowledge. The Internet has become a vast playground for collective ideas, unrestrained by decorum, undeterred by legalities, energized by exhibition, fed by potential. Easily lost in this fanfare, far from sight and mind, is the simple principle of respect for individual ownership. Idea socialism has obscured the notion that the words of an idea might actually belong to someone else.

Take for instance the emergence of several books touted, at least by their authors, for their communal creativity. Using a "there's nothing new under the sun" justification, a new genre of book borrows liberally and verbatim from blogs or blatantly repurposes other people's words, some cited, some not. This tendency, if not trend, to embezzle ideas and beliefs, reinforces the ends rather than the means.

> **US:** *So what do you think of musicians who use portions of other artist's songs, like music sampling?*
> **THEM:** *What do you mean? That happens all the time in mash-ups. What's the big deal?*
> **US:** *So you think it's okay?*
> **THEM:** *Totally. What's wrong with it?*

US: *Well, how would you feel if you made up a really cool online game, and then discovered the same game, but someone else claimed to have created it?*
THEM: *I don't know. Maybe they did. Anyway, I wouldn't care. It's all just for fun.*
US: *I guess for me, that would make me pretty angry. I'd feel like something had been taken from me without my consent. All the person had to do was acknowledge that someone else thought the game up first. It's a matter of integrity and respect for other people.*

We can't stop a trend from occurring, but once it does, we prepare ourselves, and our adolescents, to recognize it for what it is, good and bad. We question constructively so they learn how to. We let them sharpen their critical thinking skills on us even if it scratches a little. We talk about character-building tools like honesty, integrity, and respect in context so our adolescents see how to use them, how these attributes build a moral foundation. By their adolescence, we layer in our parenting, filling cracks, patching as needed. Not in big slabs, but bit by bit, in the in-betweens of conversations here and there. And then we let it harden to their cores.

TAKING RISKS GIVES THEM POWER

DURING OUR CHILDREN'S ADOLESCENCE, RISK APPEARS ON our doorsteps, uninvited, a devilish rogue determined to entice our adolescents and disrupt any remaining balance of power in the household. Rather than turn risk away as the harmful intruder that it is, we engage it head-on, involving our adolescents in the process: *Here are the issues we're concerned about.* Or *We need to know how you'll be able to stay in touch with us while you're there.* Or *We can't sanction this plan until . . .* Like fire, risk is as dangerous as it is powerful, as alluring as it is terrifying—particularly to a teenager. Only by fully understanding the powerful role that risk plays in our adolescents' lives can we teach them to read and heed its warning labels.

The Nature of Risk

ADOLESCENTS PLAY WITH RISK THE WAY TODDLERS PLAY WITH the concept of *no.* They take risks to test and probe its boundaries—and ours. Without meaningful boundaries, there would be no paths to discovery, or directions to choose. With-out risk taking, our adolescents rely on our decisions; thus the power of success remains ours. Risks related to achieve-ment, such as learning, sports, or the arts, pave the way to self-awareness and confidence, while risks that somehow backfire build much-needed resilience.

We can't prevent risk taking any more than we can pre-vent growth spurts, but we can focus on the *whether to* deci-sions surrounding each risk. By running ongoing *if-then* scenarios, like drills, we get a sense of their reasoning skills, while our adolescents get practice applying them. This way, when they stumble over real-life situations, we can point out the obstacles more easily.

Sounds like you've made a really bad decision, not to mention broken the Rules of Play. Or Did you consider the possible conse-quences of this decision? Or What do you think you should do about this . . . ? Or Want to know how others have handled these types of decisions . . . ?

The Power of Risk

WHAT BETTER LESSON FOR AN ADOLESCENT THAN TO KNOW when to take and when to avoid risk? It is not the risks them-selves that we fear most, but our adolescents' ability to cope with a veritable stampede of them, all heading in their direc-tion. We fear that they are not ready to handle the onslaught. We fear lack of consistently good judgment as the true gover-nors of their actions. We fear that our parental controls will not hold. We fear losing them as they run headlong toward a dis-tant, less forgiving future. We fear our own fear, and especially their lack of it. But what we should *not* fear is their freedom. Without freedom, adolescents have no energy source, no way to build their own power supply. No strength or courage to try new things, to confront the very risks that threaten them. That is why their power must be strong, at times even infuriating, impenetrable. That is why they must learn to rely on this power as a personal demon capable of great harm, but also great good. Only then can they wean themselves from us, their primary suppliers. Unless they occasionally test its limits, they will never know the full voltage of their power, or how to control it.

We may have begun the childrearing experiment, but its maturation steadily weakens our control while strengthening theirs. We ponder the allure of such cultural phenoms as the Wizards of Waverly Place, the merry band of Twilighters, and Harry Potter. Perhaps their true magic is not some supernatural predisposition but a willingness to take risks, make mistakes, and channel and control his personal power.

Just as a polio vaccine uses the virus to stimulate the production of antibodies, exposure to risk can actually help an adolescent recognize and even build resistance to its harmful effects. Knowing that risks permeate the life of an adolescent, we do our best to vaccinate them with a variety of risk assessment techniques. Also known as *Things to Look For*, here is an example of a risk assessment that can accompany an adolescent to a party:

- Parent or adult presence (someone to answer the door if the police come).
- Number of kids (the larger the number, the more easily it can get out of control).
- Overt presence and use of alcohol or drugs.
- Noise levels (and general rowdiness).
- Treatment of surroundings (respect for property).

Part of keeping them safe is not leaving them defenseless.

US: *You two really seem to like each other.*

THEM: *Yeah, I guess so. Is there a problem with that?*

US: *Not at all, especially if you make each other feel good about yourselves. But you know our primary concerns are safety and respect, right?*

THEM: *Yep. I know. You've only told me about a thousand times!*

US: *Good. I'm glad you remember. Now for the 1,001st time, you are still young and don't need to feel that the only way to show your feelings is to go as far as you can, or the other person wants to. There's a lot of fun to be had without getting into potentially harmful territory, like intercourse or oral sex. At your age and stage, we strongly disapprove of that level of sex.*

THEM: *Look, I know how to be careful. I know the risks! You need to trust me to be responsible!*

US: *I do trust that you understand about responsibility. But I also know how fast things can progress when two people are sexually active and enjoying themselves, especially if they really like each other. My job is to remind you of the risks, remember?* [Pause, take a breath.] *Your job is to weigh the risks and make sure that, above all, you are both prepared and comfortable. Your job is to stay safe and respect others. That means not doing anything that could harm yourself or another person.*

THEM: *Okay! I get it.*

US: *So do you have a way of getting ahold of condoms? [Or do you want me to help you make an appointment to get some birth control pills? Or do you need help getting prevention?]*

Clearly, this conversation falls into the personal conviction department. Some of us may prefer to convey our values without getting involved in tactical solutions. Others of us may want the added assurance of knowing that our adolescents have what they need to stay safe. The key is that our adolescents know what we're thinking, and we know they know even if they don't return the favor.

BALANCING THE POWER SCALES

ADOLESCENTS TAKE RISKS LIKE A GAMBLER ROLLS DICE, NEVER sure of the outcome, but thrilled by the prospects. Research based on 140 different studies of addiction and the adolescent brain concludes that the quest for the novel experience is a key driver, or motivator, of adolescent behavior.[1] We may mourn the passing of a childhood untempted by adult amusements such as drinking, driving, even smoking, but we cannot deny it. The effect of so many new impulses at play in the adolescent brain actually makes them more susceptible to addiction. In fact, most addictions to alcohol, nicotine, and drugs begin during adolescence.

As difficult and painful as adolescence can be for our overly sensitized, thoroughly self-consumed, and unfathomably self-conscious charges, it can be even harder and more unnatural for us to stand by and watch. Never before has it felt so wrong to relinquish our control. Not since infancy have our children appeared (to us) so vulnerable and so much in need of our protection. But in the adolescent quest to realign the balance of power in their lives, the more control *we* seek, the more risk we force *them* to take.

As parents, we exist first and foremost *for* our children. Otherwise, we would not *be* parents. Any satisfaction we manage to earn as a result is but an added bonus. If we do our jobs well, that satisfaction knows no bounds. Somehow, our parenting responsibilities don't shrink as our children age; they expand. If babyhood represents the dawn of our parenting day, and childhood the morning, adolescence makes for a very, very long afternoon.

By adolescence, keeping them safe, nourished, and sheltered requires constant risk assessment. While we never go off-duty as parents, in adolescence that duty requires equal doses of vigilance and faith. So as we accompany our teenagers on a long sightseeing trip through the adolescent jungle, we take every opportunity to describe the dangers, pointing out their many disguises, smells, impacts, as enticing as they are dangerous. Satisfied that our adolescents are at least aware, we do our best to monitor and assess the myriad risks they confront, painfully aware of the many temptations there for the adolescent taking.

RISKS PAST AND PRESENT

MANY OF US ACTIVELY STORE A HOST OF MEMORIES FROM our own adolescence partly in the hope that they might supply some inspiration or meaning to our parenting. Whether these memories are R-rated or PG, whether they have improved with age or been obsolesced by it, we rely on them to link a familiar past with an unfamiliar present. Some of us may even inflate our pasts to prop up a particular point of view, tattered or dated though it may be. To an adolescent, our *When I was a kid* . . . adages tend to have as much impact and interest as elevator music.

Few in our generation, which ushered rebellion into many a tidy living room, probably felt as though we had "earned a drink"—make that "earned a binge"—by Thursday night of a hard week of school. Most of us weren't cautioned to find a babysitter for our drinks at a party out of fear of random spikings with even more random substances. And *HIV* was not a household acronym; if it existed at all, adolescents certainly didn't make up the fastest-growing risk group for contracting it. Even the marijuana our adolescents use is much more potent than that which many of us developed a liking for. In the 1960s and 1970s, a joint consisted of somewhere between 1 and 5 percent THC, or tetrahydrocannabinol, the active chemical in marijuana. Today, the THC is three times that—and getting stronger.[2] Many of us can attest to surviving a host of temptations and debaucheries that checkered our own adolescence. Few of us would have predicted even greater dangers for our children.

Perhaps our pasts serve us best as a collective conscience rather than pointed reminders of a particular situation. We don't so much need to recall the specifics of the time we took LSD or "overheard" someone talking about certain test questions, but rather the gooey insides of those predicaments, the sticky parts that we can still taste and feel, if we dare: what it *felt* like the first time we got drunk and threw up; the pulsing *rush* of adrenaline mixed with fear at our first near miss in a car; the blanket of panic that *electrified* all our senses at the prospect of a potential unwanted pregnancy. These types of experiences established the roots of our compassion, one of our best opportunities to mitigate risk with our own adolescents.

> **US:** *All I can remember is how disgusting it was watching kids throw up when they drank too much . . . the way it gets in your hair and on your clothes and leaves that horrible taste in your mouth. I remember one time seeing*

*Teddy Vines throw up all over our couch. Even after we
cleaned it up, every time he came over, I was reminded of
it. Your grandmother never forgot it, either.*

As long as we admit past wrongdoings by acknowledging
them as examples of errant judgment, or cast them in terms
of lessons learned, then we don't risk oversharing. If a self-
admission feels too extreme or uncomfortable, however, then
revise accordingly.

THEM: *Are you saying you would hold it against
someone forever if they threw up in our house? What if
Grady was sleeping over and got the stomach flu and
threw up all over the carpet? You'd never forgive her?*

Rarely does an adolescent conversation follow a straight
path; rather it winds and bends, and strays off our intended
course. When this happens, we retrace our steps, trying to
avoid decoys.

US: *I understand the pressures of wanting to feel part of a
party. The thing I don't understand is how kids can drink
until they throw up and then just keep drinking. Not only
is it gross [*how we feel*], throwing up is a pretty clear
danger signal from your brain—not to mention your body's
way of purging harmful toxins [*see chapter 1, Their
Brains Are to Blame*]. By the time you vomit, damage
has already been done, plus it can be the first sign of
alcohol poisoning [*clinical reality*]. Drinking to the point
of vomiting is* not *staying safe, and if you're in someone's
home, it* certainly *isn't showing respect.*
THEM: *Whatever . . .*

Degrees of Risk

ONE OF THE EASIEST WAYS TO UNDERMINE OUR ADOLESCENTS' search for their own limits is to assert that kids will be kids; ergo, not much has changed since the raucous days of our own adolescence. This tack relies on sometimes embellished, sometimes aggrandizing descriptions of pasts involving vast quantities of alcohol (especially in states with a legal drinking age of eighteen), parentless party hunting, sexual exploits, and weed on the way to school. The motivations behind adolescent thrill seeking, such as the coolness or hipness factor, popularity, or the need for release or experience, date back generations. To deny critical differences between life as an adolescent a generation ago and now, however, denies radical differences in the incubation process of adolescence itself. Perhaps these differences can best be summed up in two words: *intensity* and *accessibility.*

Most of our lives, hence our children's lives, whirl at a much higher pitch than in our youth. The sheer number of extracurricular activities *per child* probably exceeds the totals in the generally larger families of our childhoods. After all, who says that they need to wait until ninth grade to learn algebra? Or the seventh grade to read *To Kill a Mockingbird*? Most sixth graders already know about rape and racism, don't they? Why limit their potential by having them play on a local team when they can also join a traveling team? Or two? Why wait to go to Yale for college when they can spend summers there in high school? Why take one advanced placement course when they can take three? We turn up the intensity of our expectations like heat, and assume immediate results. And so we build better cars, more advanced computers, and more capable adolescents.

By and large, our adolescents rise to the occasion, achieving more, outperforming any indices we dare consult. But at what price—and how much higher is today's price than the one we paid? To see, try a quick scan of the behaviors of our own adolescents' cohort:

- The number of R-rated movies seen by age ten.
- Bingeing by age eleven.
- Oral sex by age twelve.
- Depression by age thirteen.
- Suicide attempts by age sixteen.

To assume no link between these behaviors, and the significant increases in stress levels among eight- to seventeen-year-olds may be naïve. And some may be surprised to learn that these are not our parents' kids. It's probably safe to assume that our kids know a lot more about a lot more than we did. But how much do they understand?

> **US:** *I could tell you had been drinking when you came home last night . . .*

The evidence need not be irrefutable; a strong hunch is enough to start down this path.

> **THEM:** *You could not! I was not!*
> **US:** *That's not the discussion I want to have right now. The one I want to have has to do with how things are going with you.*
> **THEM:** *I've told you; compared to most kids, you don't need to worry. Even if I had a couple of sips, I know what I'm doing and I'm not into getting drunk. Anyway, I didn't even have a few sips. Nothing happened!*

Adolescents don't have to be innocent until proven guilty for us to assert a position. Successful parenting doesn't hinge on matching wits and counting victories; it depends on keeping the ball in play.

US: *You've been feeling a lot of pressure lately, haven't you? A lot of schoolwork and other stuff.*

THEM: *Yeah. I really want to do well this term and this is my last chance to make varsity. I'm not going to play another season of JV. It's just not going to happen.*

US: *I know how much you want these things, and I know we sometimes increase rather than help decrease your angst. I'm really worried that the more anxious you feel, the more you're going to want to try things that are supposed to alleviate the pressure, but actually only add to it.*

THEM: *Having some fun doesn't increase the pressure, it relieves it. We all need a way to blow off steam.*

US: *I know that's how risky behavior starts out. But I also know how easy it is to lose track of the number of sips or how much alcohol goes into a drink. I also understand the desire to blow off steam and try new things, but it's my job to point out the dangers and safety issues.*

THEM: *I know. I'm careful, I promise. A lot more careful than most people.* [A different track might sound something like: *Don't worry; I can handle it.*]

US: *What can we do to help? For now, let me play the bad guy. Let's say you stay home tonight, do a little homework, and get to bed early. Blame it on me.*

THEM: *No, I really want to go to Sean's party. I thought you wanted to help by decreasing the pressure. This is going to make it much worse! I knew I shouldn't have told you anything! You always say if I tell the truth, I won't get in trouble.*

US: *I know and I'm really sorry, and you're not in trouble [*and mean it because this constitutes a major whack*]. I know how much you want to go and feel you deserve to go. But I do believe that part of what you're feeling comes from an honest desire to live up to your own—and our—expectations. Sometimes, lying low, just for a night, can be a release. You just seem to be wound up pretty tightly.*
THEM: *But that's not fair! C'mon.*
US: *Sweetie, I'm sorry. But sometimes I just have to go with my gut. This one's on me.*

Sometimes good parenting requires us to play the bad guy—especially in the face of peer pressure. We can survive a few misplaced accusations better than our adolescents can.

More than ever before, our teenagers have access to almost anything they desire—if not literally, then vicariously. A recent study on teens, sex, and TV reported that 72 percent of fifteen- to seventeen-year-olds think that sexual content on TV influences *other* teens' behavior, whereas only one in four believe it influences *their* behavior specifically.[3] Research has also found that nonsmoking adolescents who saw people smoking on-screen were three times more likely to take up smoking.[4]

That our adolescents believe that oral sex is not "sex" or that vodka dispensed from Poland Spring water bottles is de rigueur at ninth-grade parties is neither an accident nor an anomaly. These beliefs simply exist as adolescent phenomena, further evidence of adolescents' inability to weigh risk and foresee outcomes *consistently*. The increase in adolescent STDs and drug and alcohol use at increasingly younger ages render comparisons to our own adolescences invalid. If fact, comparable data doesn't even exist. The back of the school bus has never been a place for the faint of heart, but only recently has it become a haven for oral sex. Though many of us strived to conceal our dabblings with marijuana, how many knew to disguise its distinctive odor by rolling it in fabric softener sheets?

From social pressures to style pressures, from the desire to measure up or just keep up, from the influence of technology to the effects of affluence, we are raising adolescents under very different conditions than we experienced. The results are not just psychological; even adolescent bodies are maturing much earlier, forcing their emotions (and brains) to play catch-up. A recent study found that 65 percent of parents of preteens and 78 percent of parents of teens recognize that adolescents today have it much harder than they themselves did.[5] Anyone who believes differently might try a dose of MTV, which has single-handedly turned adolescence into a commercial laboratory.[6]

There are many different types of risks we can, and need to, convey to our adolescents. If we attempt to download them indiscriminately or in batches, however, they invariably end up in the same scrap pile with other discarded parental misgivings. So we pick and choose, according to the moment and the opportunity.

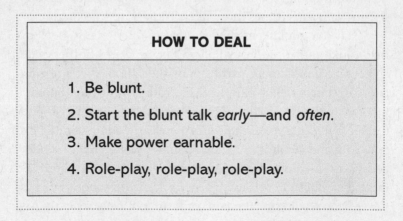

HOW TO DEAL

1. Be blunt.

2. Start the blunt talk *early*—and *often*.

3. Make power earnable.

4. Role-play, role-play, role-play.

1. Be Blunt

Many of us learned the taboos of our own adolescence through back channels, such as friends, rumors, magazines, or other such unreliable sources. Inside the walls of our own homes, any incidents involving unsavory subjects were usually whisked away, like dirty laundry, to be washed and starched before airing. Now dirty laundry *is* prime-time fare, and those old taboos belong in our generation gap, not theirs. If a topic can be accessed as readily on the nightly news as it can on the Web, shouldn't it also be welcome, or at least tolerated, in our own family chat rooms?

According to a recent study, only 4 percent of mothers are comfortable talking about sex and drugs with their adolescents.[7] A different study indicates that 98 percent of parents polled claim to discuss sex, drugs, and alcohol-related subjects with their adolescents, although only 78 percent of adolescents concur.[8]

Like it or not, if we don't start the conversation, they probably won't either.

As uncomfortable or unnatural as it feels at first, the more blunt the truth, the more real we sound, and the more likely our adolescents will listen. The very act of stepping out of character often grabs their attention.

Just listen to them with their peers. Questions and answers flow unencumbered by innuendo or accusation. Without fear of retribution, adolescents share openly and graphically with one another, often even revealing strains of parental warnings and lessons. Observations and opinions lurch from their mouths, crude and reflexive, like uninhibited belches. In that way, adolescents are the ultimate truth tellers.

For our parts, sometimes stating a worst fear out loud transforms it into a manageable concern.

US: *How was it? What did you guys do?*
THEM: *It was fine. Nothin'.*
US: *You must have done something.*
THEM: *Not really. We just hung out.*

When in doubt, pause. Accusations, however hot, dissipate quickly, if left alone. For those who haven't noticed, adolescents come equipped with a variety of defensive devices. These range from the *clamming effect* (which allows them to shut themselves off without warning or recourse), to the *dart effect* (which they use to pinpoint any remotely relevant weaknesses in us), to the *boomerang effect* (otherwise known as *the best defense is a good offense*). We recognize these tricks of the adolescent trade for what they are—and may still employ some of them ourselves!

US: *I just wondered what it was like for you. Liddy's mom mentioned she hadn't been feeling well lately.*

Although not guaranteed to work, another tactic for ferreting out information involves aimlessly ticking off names as if removing lint from a sweater. If the way seems clear, we probe even deeper: *Were Tom and Sally together? Did anyone surprising hook up?*

Nonchalantly, we knead our conversations with our adolescents like dough, massaging and reshaping, and then setting them aside to rise on their own, or not. This last step is often the hardest. If an issue doesn't involve safety, or threaten disrespect, or if it isn't vital to smooth family functioning, then *we* model impulse restraint. If an issue falls into one of the three Rules of Play categories, however, then we confront it bluntly and without hesitation.

Note: An important characteristic of blunt talk is its tone:

caring but firm, devoid of anger or disapproval. Asking questions opens doors; accusing closes them. Use a punitive tone, and the conversation will quickly devolve into useless defensiveness. The innate sense of when to push and when to move on represent the yin and yang of the parent–adolescent relationship.

> **US:** *I'm really concerned that there was drinking [or sex or drugs, or what have you] going on last night. I know that you're clear about where we stand on this, but since we can't know what you're up to every moment, I need to know that you are using good judgment. Anything happen?*

This is not about true confessions, or accusations; it's about how decisions get made and potentially dangerous situations get managed. The conversation, at this point, is also about their adherence, or not, to the Rules of Play.

> **THEM:** *Why do you always assume that there is bad stuff happening—and I'm involved in it?*
> **US:** *[Concrete but calm.] Well, in this case, here are my reasons: I could smell marijuana [or you were slurring your words when you came home last night, or I heard you throwing up, or I found a condom on the floor of the car, or I overheard you on the phone . . .].*
> **THEM:** *What, are you spying on me now? [Beware of the boomerang effect.]*
> **US:** *No, nor am I accusing you. But I am living in the same house with you, which means I'm paying attention and worrying about you. And it's my job to help you learn to make the right decisions. And [repeat the reason] is not showing respect for the Rules of Play.*

2. Start the Blunt Talk *Early*—and *Often*

Parents of younger adolescents often wonder when and where to begin the blunt talk. The answer is when they are no longer content to watch or listen to a teen idol, but want to look like him or her as well (which can start as early as age ten or eleven). For adolescents, the question of *whether or not* quickly morphs into *why not?* The more straightforward our responses, the greater the chance that our values will get hardwired into an adolescent's rapidly growing brain (see chapter 1, Their Brains Are to Blame). The weaker our responses, the less our adolescents will depend on us as reliable sources. The longer we wait, the harder it is for them to find space for our opinions amid the competition.

> **THEM:** *But everyone is sleeping over, and Mr. and Mrs. Jones will both be there. If they think it's safe, why can't you?*
> **US:** *It's not what they think; it's what we think, and I know that doesn't always seem fair but it's what you have to live with as a member of this family.*

A little compassion goes a long way in dispelling the sometimes bitter taste of parental discretion. They don't have to like all of our reasons, but it helps if they understand them.

> **THEM:** *But nothing is going to happen! You want me to stay safe; it's safer to stay there than for you or someone else to be driving me around late at night!*
> **US:** *Tell me again why you think staying is safer.*

Note that *no* was not the automatic response. Allowing them to make their case offers a sneak peek into their reasoning powers and helps locate any fault lines in their adolescent logic. We then use the three Rules of Play not to lecture or moralize or threaten but to simplify.

> **THEM:** *Because it's safe. This way nobody needs to be out driving late. Why can't you trust me? We'd all just fall asleep in the basement watching movies. What do you think? We're going to have an orgy? Everybody has coed sleepovers. It's no big deal! C'mon, pleeeease? Just this once?*

Once an adolescent storm cloud forms, it builds quickly, as if fed by its own energy. Remain calm and the storm will pass (although the cloud itself may linger).

> **US:** *Although we didn't have coed sleepovers when I was a kid [trickle, don't pour, history], I do know that we're all more vulnerable in the middle of the night. Here's the type of thing I'm worried about: What happens if two people lying right next to you start hooking up in a way that makes you uncomfortable? Or someone comes on to you and you're not comfortable?*

The more blunt the descriptors, the better. By initiating the words or thoughts, we grant *them* permission to speak freely (*I know it's weird to hear me talk about this stuff, but . . .*). These kinds of admissions can take the edge off—both for them and us:

But do you know that even the smallest cut in your mouth could infect you with the AIDS virus from oral sex? Or Do you realize *that you can get pregnant if the boy ejaculates but doesn't enter the vagina?* If a relevant example exists, use it.

Too graphic to even contemplate? It might help to know that a study found that 96 percent of adolescents reported that open communication with their parents helped prevent the use of drugs, and 80 percent said that clear consequences prevented repeat behaviors.[9]

It's also okay to model a strong gut instinct as a worthy guide.

> **THEM:** *C'mon, pleeeeeease? Just this once?*
> **US:** *You know, honey, I just don't feel comfortable with this right now. It's not that I don't believe or trust you, I do. But my gut is telling me to wait. I'm sorry, because I know you're disappointed. But this is the best explanation I can offer. I'm not saying no lightly—or forever—just right now.*

If we know that the two best deterrents for risk taking in adolescence are connectedness (to us) and our disapproval, then let's try to determine our individual level of connectedness with our adolescents. Try the little assessment below:

HOW WELL DO WE KNOW OUR ADOLESCENTS?

How well do we know the following? Using the scale below as a guide, rate your level of familiarity, with a 5 indicating *extreme familiarity,* down to a 1 meaning *not at all familiar.*

Extremely familiar   5   4   3   2   1   *Not at all familiar*

a. Our adolescents' friends.

b. Their friends' friends.

c. Their friends' families.

d. The TV, movies, videogames they're watching (not just the names, but the content as well).

e. What their Facebook pages look like.

f. The Internet sites they frequent.

g. What they're doing in their spare time.

(We might be surprised at the results.)

If, after an honest and open conversation with our adolescents, the answer to a request (such as attending a coed sleepover) is *no*, then the *no* decision reflects careful consideration and communicates a resolution. The secret here is to shift the conversation away from the *no* itself to the reasons behind our disapproval. We all have the power, and the right, to say *no*. (If they question that, then reread The Rules of Play in Part I.) But a *no* based only on a desire to control is weightless. *No* might mean having to say you're sorry, but it also means trying to avoid giving your adolescent the grounds to say, *But that's not fair!*

Let's return to the conversation about attending a coed sleepover, and try another angle.

US: *Although we didn't have coed sleepovers when I was a kid, I do know that we're all more vulnerable in the middle of the night. Here's the type of thing I'm worried about: I know hooking up can be fun. If it's dark and private, it can be easier to keep going than to stop. Leaving aside for a moment [but only for a moment] whether or not you're protected, you're in a place and position that makes it very*

*hard to evaluate the risks and your feelings. I'm not saying
sex is bad, especially kissing. I'm saying that putting
yourself in a situation where sex is the easy thing to do is
bad. And it's my job to help to ensure that you don't end
up in situations that pose needless risks.*

While many risks extend beyond our reach, many do not;
many we even overlook either out of convenience or because
they are so obvious as to be invisible. Examples of these types
of risks include leaving adolescents alone in the house together day or night, unsupervised access to liquor or prescription drugs, lack of accountability, and so forth. We accept
the fact that the physiology of their growing brains sometimes
prevents our teenagers from as careful a sorting of the different types of risks as we might like. So we work to neutralize
these risk-taking proclivities with equal doses of precaution
(see chapter 1, Their Brains Are to Blame).

3. Make Power Earnable

Think of adolescence as a seven- to ten-year pilgrimage to
self-discovery. As a major benefactor of this endeavor, our
support is both crucial and varied. One of our most valuable
forms of assistance comes from the responsibilities we assign.

Well before the physical signs of adolescence confirm its
presence, we begin to recognize the reemergence, albeit in an
evolved state, of such familiar toddlerhood ploys as psychological tugs-of-war, nuanced *nos,* and dared defiance. This
time around, rather than reassert our omnipotence, we transfer it. Not outright and not automatically. We make power
earnable, choice by choice, decision by decision, never com-
promising safety or values, but rewarding responsible behavior
with increased responsibility—in increments. The more trust

our adolescents bank, the more responsibility we invest, the more self-reliance they reap. And so the earning cycle goes, until one day, no longer dependent on us, they are able to support themselves.

> **THEM:** *I'm going over to Renny's house. See you later!*
> **US:** *Sounds great! I assume your chores are finished?*
> **THEM:** *No, but I promise I'll finish later.*
> **US:** *Sorry. You know the deal; it's your responsibility to finish before you go.*
> **THEM:** *But I'm late. A bunch of people are waiting for me. I'll finish later! C'mon. You never said I had to finish before I left.*
> **US:** *I shouldn't have to; you know the deal.*
> **THEM:** *But I can't do them now! I told everybody I'd be there in ten minutes!*
> **US:** *It's up to you. Just know that if you choose to go before you complete your responsibilities, then you can expect repercussions when you get back. It's your choice . . .*

Don't feel compelled to produce a repercussion on demand; just be sure to have one ready if needed later. Immediacy is less important than follow-through.

> **THEM:** *How about this? How about I do the dishes and take out the trash now—that's all the stuff you can see. Then, later, as soon as I come back, I'll fold my laundry. I'll even fold your laundry! Now, c'mon, you know that's a good deal!*

Too often, we mistake our adolescents' desire to negotiate for an attempt to manipulate and resist. Some of us even regard negotiating as a sign of parental weakness, tantamount to being held hostage. But we are not at war with our own children, and they are certainly not the enemy.

Anyone who has successfully negotiated to *yes* has felt the power of a winning argument. Any negotiation that allows an adolescent to use responsibility to fulfill its terms is a deal we should consider. To reject it outright robs them of an invaluable opportunity to prove to themselves—and to us—that they have the power to control outcomes in beneficial ways.

4. Role-Play, Role-Play, Role-Play

Adolescents are as awkward and gangly with their words as they are with their growing limbs, constantly tripping over unformed ideas, groping for the right thing to say to win approval and acceptance (which accounts, at least in part, for the invasion of the word *like* into their vocabulary). One way to help bring order to their chaotic thought processes is to role-play with them. Just as we used to fill many empty childhood moments with *I Spy with My Little Eye* games, curious about their observational acuity, we use *What Would You Do If* role-plays to evaluate our adolescents' risk assessment powers and the relative influence of the Rules of Play. The more unstructured or unsure their responses, the more we need to clarify and reinforce our positions.

> **US:** *Have you thought about how you're going to respond when you're offered a joint or a beer? What might you say?*
> **THEM:** *I* know *what to say.* [We listen as much to the words presenting the logic as the logic itself.]
> **US:** *So what would you say?* [Step lightly.]
> **THEM:** *It depends, I guess.*

We accept an honest attempt not to lie outright for what it is. Aware that threats will only drive them further underground, we reinforce our values and the Rules of Play. As always, our best opportunity for influence and credibility is by example. Many behaviors, like language, are born from mimicry—and mimicry knows no bounds, only actions.

US: *Want to hear what other kids have said?*
THEM: *Do I have a choice?* [They know when they don't.]
US: *Some say, "Not right now," or "Maybe later," or even a nonchalant "No thanks."*
THEM: *How do you know what other kids say?*
US: *Experience. I know a lot of things that might surprise you.*

We position our suggestions as conversational tidbits rather than prescriptions or orders, hoping that our adolescents will sort them for usable morsels.

THEM: *You sound like you're at a birthday party or something. Look, I've got it under control; I told you, I'm not a drinker! And if I don't want something, I just say no. It's no big deal.*
US: *That's great. I believe you.*
TRANSLATION: *Respect goes both ways; when in doubt, err on the side of showing it.*
US: *But sometime it helps to think through some responses.*

We stage hypothetical situations as rehearsals of many real-life temptations, improvising situations, calling the question when needed. The story lines themselves evolve and adapt to reflect the current dilemma, worst fear of the day, or story of the week. The most effective role-plays blend into actual conversations—flavoring, but not necessarily dominating, them. We launch our little message missiles with nonexplosive phrases like *Ever tried . . . ? Have you ever wondered . . . ? What if he had . . . ?* And then we listen to the response, planning our next probe, not so much to interrogate as to understand. We don't criticize but float ideas, like bubbles, light but reflective.

Adolescents career toward adulthood as erratically and unstably as a baby learning to walk, lurching, stutter-stepping, determined to press on, unaware and unconcerned with any impediments in their path. With each step, they gain more power. With power comes self-assurance and the determination to continue. *Watch out!* we continually caution, encouraging them while begging them to slow down. But they are too engrossed in their own contradictions to notice ours. Anyway, they've heard them all before, or should have.

One by one, our adolescents learn to hurdle different risks, powered by their own curiosity, their own impulses. We watch with a mix of pride and disbelief, anticipating falls, but not necessarily trying to prevent them.

NOTES

THE RULES OF PLAY

1. "2008 Report Card: The Ethics of American Youth," Josephson Institute of Ethics, Press Release and Data Summary (2008), www.josephsoninstitute.org.

2. Dan Kindlon, Ph.D., *Too Much of a Good Thing* (New York: Hyperion, 2001), 177.

3. Traffic Safety Facts, 2008 Data, http://www-nrd.nhtsa.dot.gov/Pubs/811169.pdf.

4. Patrick M. O'Malley and Lloyd D. Johnston, University of Michigan, Institute for Social Research, "Drugs and Driving by American High School Seniors, 2001–2006," http://druggeddriving.org/duid/monitoring_druggeddriving01-6.pdf.

5. Partnership for a Drug Free America, "Partnership Attitude Tracking Study (PATS) Teen Drug and Alcohol Use Headed In Wrong Direction," http://www.drugfree.org/newsroom/new-research=teen-drug-and-alcohol-use-headed-in-wrong-direction.

6. National Survey of American Attitudes on Substance Abuse XIV: Teens and Parents, August 2009.

7. "Sexually Transmitted Diseases in the United States, 2008," www.cdc.gov/std/stats08/trends.htm.

8. L. Remez, "Oral Sex Among Adolescents: Is It Sex or Is It Abstinence?" *Family Planning Perspectives* 32:6 (November–December 2000), www.guttmacher.org.

9. "Oral Versus Vaginal Sex Among Adolescents: Perceptions, Attitudes, and Behaviors, *Pediatrics* 115:4, (April 2005), 845–851.

10. *HIV/AIDS Update,* Centers for Disease Control (December 2000).

11. Sexual and Reproductive Health of Persons Aged 10–24 Years—United States, 2002–2007, http://www.cdc.gov/mmWR/PDF/ss/ss5806.pdf.

12. "Tracking the Hidden Epidemics: Trends in STDs in the United States 2000,"www.cdc.gov/nchstp/dstd/Stats_Trends.

13. M. Mason, "Study: Screening Teen Girls for Chlamydia Could Lower Infertility,"Associated Press (December 11, 2002).

14. "A National Survey of 15 to 17 Year Olds," Kaiser Family Foundation/ MTV/Teen People (March 8, 1999): 4, www.kff.org/content/archive/ 1465/stds_t.pdf.

15. "Briefly," National Campaign to Prevent Teen Pregnancy (January 2010), www.teenpregnancy.org/resources/pdf/Briefly_Teen-Pregnancy-and-Childrearing-Teen-Headlines.pdf.

16. C. G. Andrews, "Are Parents in the Know?" citing Bradford Brown's research in *On Wisconsin* (fall 2003): 15.

1

1. Jay Giedd, interview, "Inside the Teenage Brain," *Frontline* (2002), www.pbs.org/wgbh/pages/frontline/shows/teenbrain/interviews/ giedd.html.

2. As cited in A. M. White, "Substance Use and Adolescent Brain Development: An Overview of Recent Findings with a Focus on Alcohol" (2002),www.duke.edu/~amwhite/adolescence.html.

3. T. A. Slotkin, "Nicotine and the Adolescent Brain: Insights from an Animal Model," *Neurotoxicology and Teratology* 24 (2002): 369–384.

4. Leslie Jacobsen, *Biological Psychiatry* 57 (January 2005).

5. Brenda Patoine, "Teen Brain's Ability to Learn Can Have a Flip Side," The Dana Foundation (November 2007).

6. Matt Viser, "Wake-Up Call for High Schools," *Boston Globe* (May 4, 2003): 1.

7. Siri Carpenter, "Sleep Deprivation May Be Undermining Teen Health," *Monitor on Psychology* 32 (2001): 42–45.

8. *Journal of Sleep Research.* Volume 13, September, 2004, Issue Supplement s1.

9. Pew Internet and American Life Project, Teens and Mobile Phones, April 20, 2010, http://www.pewinternet.org/~/media/Files/Reports/2010/PIP-Teens-and-Mobile-2010-with-topline.pdf.

10. Columbia University Medical Center, "Study Links Later Parental-Mandated Bedtimes for Teens with Depression and Suicidal Thoughts," June 9, 2009, http://www.cumc.columbia.edu/news/press_releases/Parental-Mandated_Bedtimes.html.

11. Amy R. Wolfson and Mary A. Carskadon, "Sleep Schedules and Daytime Functioning in Adolescents," *Child Development* 69:4: 875–887.

12. Russell D. Romeo, *Stress and the Adolescent Brain,* Laboratory of Neuroendocrinology, Rockefeller University, New York (2006).

13. Partnership for a Drug-Free America, Partnership Attitude Tracking Study, "Teen Drug and Alcohol Use Headed In Wrong Direction."

14. Gary Small, *iBrain* (New York: HarperCollins, 2008), 16.

15. Maryanne Wolf, *Proust and the Squid: The Story and Science of the Reading Brain* (New York: HarperCollins, 2007).

16. R. Kawashima, *Train Your Brain: 60 Days to a Better Brain* (Teaneck, NJ: Kumon Publishing North America, 2005).

2

1. "The Ethics of American Youth: A Report Card on Students' Values, Attitudes, and Behavior," 2008 Report Card, http://josephsoninstitute.org/surveys/index.html.

2. National Survey of American Attitudes on Substance Abuse XIV, *Teens and Parents,* August 2009.

3

1. S. Chess and A. Thomas, "Temperamental Categories and Their Definitions," in *Temperament in Clinical Practice,* Chess and Thomas, eds. (New York: Guilford, 1986), 273–281.

4

1. www.childstats.gov/americaschildren/health4.asp.

2. http://www.cdc.gov/HealthyYouth/yrbs/pdf/yrbs07_us_suicide_related_behaviors_trend.pdf.

3. www.nimh.nih.gov./research/suifact.htm.

4. *Suicide Among Children, Adolescents, and Young Adults—United States, 1980–1992* 44:15 (April 21, 1995): 289–291, www.cdc.gov/mmwr/preview/mmwrhtml/00036818.html.

5. www.teen-matters.com/bodyimage.html.

6. www.pbs.org/wgbh/pages/frontline/shows/cool/.

7. Concentration of media ownership globally, http://en.wikipedia.org/wiki/Concentration_of_media_ownership, 2008.

8. www.marketingcharts.com/interactive/teen-market-to-surpass-2011-despite-population-decline-817/.

9. www.pbs.org/wgbh/pages/frontline/shows/cool/.

10. www.marketingcharts.com/interactive/teen-market-to-surpass-2011-despite-population-decline-817/.

11. "I've Got a Feeling," The Black Eyed Peas, David Guetta, Frédéric Riesterer, 2009.

12. "2002 Report Card: The Ethics of American Youth," Josephson Institute of Ethics, Press Release and Data Summary (2002), www.josephsoninstitute.org.

13. Foster Cline and Jim Fay, *Parenting with Love and Logic: Teaching Children Responsibility* (Golden, Colo.: Love and Logic Institute, 1990).

14. Jessica Portner, *One in Thirteen: The Silent Epidemic of Teen Suicide* (Beltsville, Md.: Robins Lane Press, 2001).

15. SADD, Unpublished data from Teens Today survey.

16. http://www.psychologytoday.com/blog/freedom-learn/201001/the-dramatic-rise-anxiety-and-depression-in-children-and-adolescents-is-it.

17. http://www.apa.org/monitor/2010/01/stress-kids.aspx.

18. "Making Kids Work on Goals (And Not Just Soccer)," *Wall Street Journal,* March 9, 2011.

19. *Journal of Child Psychology and Psychiatry* 49:12 (2008): 1257–1269.

5

1. Kaiser Family Foundation, *Generation M2: Media in the Lives of 8-to-18-Year Olds,* News Release (January 2010), http://www.kff.org/entmedia/entmedia012010nr.cfm.

2. *Text Messaging Becomes Centerpiece Communication,* Pew Internet & American Life Project, April 20, 2010, http://pewresearch.org/pubs/1572/teens-cell-phones-text-messages.

3. Kaiser Family Foundation, *Generation M2: Media in the Lives of 8-to-18 Year-Olds,* News Release (January 2010), http://www.kff.org/entmedia/entmedia012010nr.cfm.

4. Ibid.

5. Ibid.

6. *Text Messaging Becomes Centerpiece Communication,* Pew Internet & American Life Project, April 20, 2010 http://pewresearch.org/pubs/1572/teens-cell-phones-text-messages.

7. Earth Policy Institute, "US Car Fleet Shrank by Four Million in 2009," www.earth-policy.org.

8. http://www.istrategylabs.com/2011/01/facebook-demographics-and-statistics-report-2011.

9. SADD (Students Against Destructive Decisions) and Liberty Mutual Corporation, "Road Map to Adolescent Decision Making" *SADD in the News* (October 29, 2002), www.saddonline.com/snews.html.

10. Ron Taffel, *The Second Family* (New York: St. Martin's Press, 2001), 36.

11. Kaiser Family Foundation, "Teens Say Sex on TV Influences Behavior of Peers: Some Positive Effects Seen," Press Release (publication 3229, May 20, 2002), www.kff.org/content/2002/3229/TeensSexTVNew Release.pdf.

12. Partnership for a Drug Free America, "2008 Partnership Attitude Tracking Study (PATS)" (February 2009), www.drugfree.org/Portal/About/News Releases/20th_Annual_Teen_Study.

13. Ibid.

14. Kaiser Family Foundation, "National Survey of Teens: Teens Talk About Dating, Intimacy, and Their Sexual Experiences" (November 1997), www.kff.org/content/archive/1373/datingrep4.html.

15. The National Campaign to Prevent Teen Pregnancy, *With One Voice: America's Adults and Teens Sound Off About Teen Pregnancy* (Washington, D.C.: National Campaign to Prevent Teen Pregnancy, 2009).

16. 4parents.gov, "Some Facts About Teen Sex" (August 2009).

17. Kaiser Family Foundations, "U.S. Teen Sexual Activity" (January 2005), www.kff.org/youthhivstds/upload/u-s-teen-sexual-activity-fact-sheet.pdf

18. Dan Kindlon, Ph.D., *Too Much of a Good Thing* (New York: Hyperion, 2001), 217.

6

1. Deborah Roffman, *The Thinking Parent's Guide to Talking Sense About Sex* (Cambridge, Mass.: Perseus, 2001).

2. "When and Why Teens Choose Drinking, Drugs and Sex," Liberty Mutual and SADD, Executive Summary (2002), www.saddonline.com.

3. Ibid.

4. "14 and Younger: The Sexual Behavior of Young Adolescents," National Campaign to Prevent Teen Pregnancy (May 2003), www.teenpregnancy.org.

5. National Longitudinal Study of Adolescent Health, Carolina Population Center at University of North Carolina (1998).

6. S. S. Luthar, D. Cicchetti, and B. Becker, "The Construct of Resilience: A Critical Evaluation and Guidelines for Future Work," *Child Development* 70 (2000): 543–562.

7. Juliet Chung, "Less than Half of Teens Think Their Schools Are Free of Drugs," *Wall Street Journal* (August 20, 2003), citing a survey conducted by the National Center on Addiction and Substance Abuse at Columbia University.

8. Teen Today Report (2001), www.saddonline.com.

9. Kate Zernike, "Teens Want More Advice from Parents on Sex," *New York Times* (December 16, 2003), http://www.teenpregnancy.org/about/announcements/news/pdf/NY%20Times%2012-16-03.pdf.

10. L. R. Huesmann, J. Moise-Titus, C, Podolski, and L. D. Eron, "Longitudinal Relations Between Children's Exposure to TV Violence

and Their Aggressive and Violent Behavior in Young Adulthood: 1977–1992," *Developmental Psychology* 39:2 (2003): 201–221

11. Alex Kuczynski, "She's Got to Be a Macho Girl," *New York Times* (November 3, 2002).

12. J.G. Silverman, A. Raj, L. Mucci, and J. E. Hathaway, "Dating Violence Against Adolescent Girls and Associated Substance Use, Unhealthy Weight Control, Sexual Risk Behavior, Pregnancy, and Suicidality," *Journal of the American Medical Association* 286:5 (2001): 572–579.

13. P. Tjaden and N. Thoennes, *National Violence Against Women Survey* (Washington, D.C.: U.S. Department of Justice, National Institute of Justice, Centers for Disease Control and Prevention, 1998).

14. Centers for Disease Control and Prevention, "Youth Risk Behavior Surveillance—United States, 2007 (June 2008), http://www.mcph.org/Major_Activities/MHPRC/IM/2008/IM608/NEWS_YRBS_2007_Summary.pdf.

15. Erica Noonan, "Parents Crucial Amid Affluence, Angst," *Boston Globe* (February 9, 2003).

16. "With One Voice (lite)," A 2009 Survey of Adults and Teens on Parental Influence, Abstinence, Contraception, and the Increase in the Teen Birth Rate, http://www.thenationalcampaign.org/resources/pdf/pubs/WOV_Lite_2009.pdf.

17. Zernike.

18. Letter to parents, Robert P. Henderson Jr. of Nobles and Greenough School, citing Thayer Academy headmaster Eric Swaim.

19. The National Campaign to Prevent Teen and Unplanned Pregnancy, Sex and Tech Survey (2008), www.thenationalcampaign.org/sextech/PDF/SexTech_Summary.pdf.

20. Pew Internet & American Life Project, "Online Privacy: What Teens Share and Restrict in an Online Environment."

21. *New York Times,* "Rethinking Sex Offender Laws for Youth Texting," March 20, 2010.

22. *New York Times,* The Web Means the End of Forgetting," July 21, 2010.

23. Pew Internet & American Life Project, "Online Privacy: What Teens Share and Restrict in an Online Environment."

7

1. R. A. Chamber, J. R. Taylor, and M. C. Potenza, "Developmental Neurocircuitry of Motivation in Adolescence: A Critical Period of Activation Vulnerability," *American Journal of Psychiatry* 160 (June 2003): 1041–1052.

2. Michael J. Bradley, Ed.D., *Yes, Your Teen Is Crazy!* (Gig Harbor, Wash.: Harbor Press, 2002), 290.

3. Kaiser Family Foundation and *U.S. News & World Report,* "Teens, Sex, TV Survey" (April 2002), www.kff.org/content/2002/3229/TeensSex TVNewsRelease.pdf.

4. M. A. Dalton, J. D. Sargent, M. L. Beach, L. Titus-Ernstoff, J. J. Gibson, M. B. Ahrens, J. J. Tickle, and T. F. Heatherton, "Effect of Viewing Smoking in Movies on Adolescent Smoking Initiation: A Cohort Study," *Lancet* 362:9380 (July 2003): 281–285.

5. Nickelodeon, Kaiser Family Foundation, and Kids Now, "Talking with Kids About Tough Issues: A National Survey of Parents and Kids" (December 2000–January 2001), www.kff.org/content/2001/3107/ summary.pdf.

6. R. McChesney, quoted in "The Symbiotic Relationship Between the Media and Teens," Merchants of Cool, *Frontline* (February 27, 2001), www.pbs.org/wgbh/pages/frontline/shows/cool/themes/symbiotic.html.

7. R. W. Blum, "Teen Sexuality and the Role of Communication and Decision-making," *Healthy Teen Development* (Iowa State University: National Satellite Series, October 24, 2002), www.extension.iastate.edu/ teen/facilitator/blum.pdf.

8. SADD and Liberty Mutual, "2001 Teens Today Report Shatters the Myth of Inevitability," http://www.saddonline.com/teenstoday.htm#chart4: 19.

9. Ibid.

SELECTED REFERENCES

Bradley, Michael J., Ed.D. *Yes, Your Teen Is Crazy!* Gig Harbor, Wash.: Harbor Press, 2002.

Di Prisco, Joseph, and Michael Riera. *Field Guide to the American Teenager.* Cambridge, Mass.: Perseus Publishing, 2000.

Rosemond, John. *Teen-Proofing.* Kansas City: Andrews McMeel Publishing, 2001.

Taffel, Ron. *The Second Family.* New York: St. Martin's Press, 2001.

Tolman, Deborah. *Dilemmas of Desire.* Cambridge, Mass.: Harvard University Press, 2002.

Jenifer Marshall Lippincott has worked with adolescents for more than two decades as a teacher, dean, and learning consultant. She holds a master's degree in human development from Harvard University. She lives in Washington, D.C., with her husband and two adolescent daughters.

Robin M. Deutsch, Ph.D., is the Director of the Center of Excellence for Children, Families and the Law at the Massachusetts School of Professional Psychology, a consultant in the Department of Psychiatry at Massachusetts General Hospital, and an associate clinical professor at Harvard Medical School. In her psychology practice she sees children, adolescents, and parents. She successfully survived the adolescence of a son and a daughter.